THE
RELUCTANT
ENTREPRENEUR:

Making a Living Doing What You Love

Mary Ellen Bates

Niwot Press

Niwot Press

Published by Niwot Press
8494 Boulder Hills Drive, Niwot, Colorado 80503

Cover Design by Brain Bolts
www.BrainBolts.com

Library of Congress Control Number: 2014907116

ISBN: 978-0-615-97595-5

Also by Mary Ellen Bates

Building & Running a Successful Research Business

Super Searchers Cover the World

Researching Online for Dummies

Mining for Gold on the Internet

Super Searchers Do Business

The Online Deskbook

To my wife, Lin Harden, who enriches my life every day, and to the memory of my parents, Pete and Flo Bates, who taught me to be fearless.

CONTENTS

Introduction

Alice: Would you tell me, please, which way
I ought to go from here?
Cheshire Cat: That depends a good deal
on where you want to get to.

LEWIS CARROLL, FROM *ALICE'S ADVENTURES IN WONDERLAND*

One of my favorite magazines is Scientific American; every month I expand my understanding of some aspect of our world. I have noticed that the articles about animals often refer to how they "make a living"—find a place to sleep, find food, avoid being eaten, and protect their family. Clearly, I had always looked at the idea of making a living far too narrowly. Yes, it involves finding a way to provide for myself and my family, but it also includes how I live my life—whether I experience life as predator or prey, whether I see my resources as abundant or scarce, whether I feel threatened or brave.

This book offers you a way to make a living while still enjoying life—not just bringing home a paycheck but also creating a living doing what feeds your spirit and enriches you. I share with you my approach to building a business that reflects who you are and what you enjoy doing, week after week, year after year. Being an entrepreneur is the best job I've ever had, and the scariest. I have done things that were far outside my comfort zone. I have come face to face with my biggest character flaws as well as some unexpected strengths. And I cannot imagine having it any other way.

I confess that I didn't wake up one morning and suddenly wish that I were running my own business. I liked what I was doing well enough—I ran the library of a *Fortune* 500 company—and my employer was OK. Eventually, though, I realized that my career path would likely involve managing more and more people, having more administrative responsibilities, and not doing as much research, which was what I loved to do. Back in 1991 when I was attending a professional conference, I stopped by the booth of an association of people, many of whom were former librarians, who ran their own research businesses and who were collegial and welcoming. This group, the Association of Independent Information Professionals (aiip.org), gave me much-needed encouragement and support as I quit my full-time job and launched Bates Information Services.

The first couple of years were challenging; I needed to learn most of my lessons the hard way, so I found out by trial and error all the ways *not* to move a business forward. I tried cold-calling. I tried direct mail. I tried advertising. I tried discounting my rate. Then I decided that, since all the traditional methods weren't working, I might as well create my own approach. I started building the "Mary Ellen Bates" brand by acting like the confident business owner I hoped to someday become. I started soliciting speaking opportunities, even though I was terrified at the thought of speaking in public. I told myself that, as scary as giving a speech would be, it would still be better than working in a cubicle, dealing with office politics, and being miserable.

Eventually, I found that most of the things that initially felt impossible were easier than I had anticipated. I was highly motivated to find a way to earn a living without working for someone else, but I found it challenging to see myself as a (ahem) Business Owner. My approach to strategic planning was a strange combination of NASA and Malcolm X. Failure was simply not an option, and I was going to figure out a way to build a successful business by any—legal and ethical, although probably scary—means necessary. The result has been a business that has sustained me for most of my professional life, that has enabled me to expand my vision of myself and my business, and that is rewarding both financially and energetically.

I wrote this book for people who really love what they do and want to find a way to be of service to others and make a living in the process. It's for therapists, consultants, financial planners, home inspectors, graphic designers—anyone who has a gift, a passion, something unique they want to share with the world. My focus is on people who have a professional service they want to offer rather than businesses that make products. The development, design, production, and shipping of physical products involve serious capital and a complex network that goes beyond this book. Likewise, if your dream is to open a café or retail store, you're looking for more than what I cover here. And for the sake of simplicity, I've written this book from the perspective of an American working in the United States. Many of the ideas and approaches apply outside the United States as well; if you are a non-U.S. reluctant entrepreneur, take from this book what you find most useful and ignore whatever doesn't resonate with you.

In fact, that's good advice for every reader. I offer my perspective on how we reluctant—or at least not wildly enthusiastic—entrepreneurs can have fun make a living, based on my own experience and that of hundreds of my fellow entrepreneurs. Some of what you read will ring true, some will sound challenging, and some may strike you as counterintuitive or downright crazy. I encourage you to try everything that sounds possible (note that I didn't say "easy") and that feels like it reflects the authentic you, as big as you can imagine yourself.

In Chapter One, *But I'm Not an Entrepreneur*, I begin by helping you think about what makes you unique—what is your special combination of talent, passion, and expertise that no one else has? I also give you some questions to consider, to help you figure out how comfortable you will be as a business owner.

Chapter Two, *The Joys and Frustrations of Being an Entrepreneur*, gives you a basic reality check on what it's really like to be self-employed. You may be surprised by some of the unexpected benefits; in fact, you may find that you actually enjoy doing things that initially sounded intimidating or downright impossible. Among the downsides of being your own boss, the most challenging may be learning how to think of yourself as a business (as well as the wonderful human being you know you are).

You will find some guidance on shifting your perspective in Chapter Three, *The Mind of an Entrepreneur*. I help you move from the mindset of a freelancer to that of a business owner. I look at the "Imposter Syndrome," in which you wonder when people are going to realize what a fraud you really are. And I offer some tools to help you become the confident, competent business owner that you know you can be.

Chapter Four, *Who Are Your Clients?*, challenges you to think beyond what you think your clients want, and to find out what they really value. I show you how to conduct what I call "reality-check interviews," during which you learn what your prospective clients' biggest concerns are and how you can build a business around addressing those concerns.

Only after you figure out who your clients are do I get into Chapter Five, *Building the Framework*. Here, I offer options on how you can structure your business—as a sole proprietor, a corporation, a limited liability company (LLC), or a partnership. And, while I am not a big fan of formal business plans, I include a series of questions to help you think through the key elements of getting your business off the ground.

Many people find that one of the most challenging aspects of being self-employed is managing themselves. Chapter Six, *Managing Yourself and Your Business*, covers how to create a healthy work/life balance, how to stay sharp and keep focused, and how to keep a wide-open perspective on what's possible with your business and your life.

Take a deep breath before you dive into Chapter Seven, *All About Money*. As much as we would like people to just throw hundred dollar bills at us, most business owners also learn how to think about money in new ways. This chapter helps you figure out how much to charge for your services, how to get paid by your clients, and how to keep your cash flow flowing.

Of course, you can't have much of a business without clients, and Chapter Eight, *The Care and Feeding of Clients*, covers how to manage your clients, how to deal with problem clients, and even how to fire a client. After all, what's the point of being an entrepreneur if you have to work with people you don't like?

No one enjoys cold calling, and Chapter Nine, *Your (Fabulous) Marketing Plan*, shows you how you can build your business by attracting rather than chasing after clients. Your marketing plan will provide you with tangible goals, clear progress markers, and strategies to get the most value from your marketing efforts.

Chapter Ten, *Brand "You,"* shows you how to look at yourself from your client's perspective and describe yourself in a way that effectively conveys your value. My strategies on how to build and promote Brand "You" will help you build a base of loyal clients who know how great you are and why they should call you again and again.

And finally, Chapter Eleven, *The Reluctantly Strategic Entrepreneur*, gives you tools for ensuring that your business continues to thrive as you continue to discover what your clients value the most and what you enjoy doing. No business that stays stagnant can survive, and this chapter helps you continue to evolve naturally.

As you can see, this book isn't for people who just want a self-funding hobby or a tax deduction; it's for those of us who are willing to extend our comfort zone in order to create a sustaining business. We want to make a good living, but we don't need to build a dynasty that will fund our grandchildren's trust funds. We just want to wake up in the morning and look forward to going into the office, especially if the office is just down the hall from the bedroom.

Prepare to be challenged, energized, and encouraged as you learn how to create a business you love.

1 But I'm Not an Entrepreneur

> Mad Hatter: Have I gone mad?
> Alice: I'm afraid so. You're entirely bonkers.
> But I'll tell you a secret. All the best people are.
>
> FROM *ALICE IN WONDERLAND* (TIM BURTON FILM, 2010)

What do you think of when you hear the word entrepreneur? Do you imagine someone who is driven to succeed, who always has a fistful of business cards ready to hand out, and whose goal is to earn a million dollars a year before he turns thirty?

Entrepreneurs share a love of what they do and a willingness to move beyond their comfort zone.

Actually, there are lots of people who are quietly creating a fulfilling life, doing what they love and working for themselves. They probably would not call themselves entrepreneurs, and their biggest ambition is to make a good living and have fun in the process, not wondering what new competitor they can vanquish. They left the world of employment, whether voluntarily or not, and have found ways—however reluctantly—to find and keep customers, handle bookkeeping, and keep the lights on at home. What they have in common is their love of what they do and their willingness to move beyond their comfort zone as they learn how to make a living in a new way.

What Does an Entrepreneur Look Like?

Entrepreneurs come in many forms and packages. When I needed to install a fence for my yard, I learned that there are fence brokers, people who meet with the customer to find out her particular fencing needs and then shop the job to a selected network of reputable fence installers. The fence broker selects the best bid, adds his fee, and I get a new fence. The fence brokers get their business from word-of-mouth referrals, and their network of installers gets its business by providing reliably excellent work at a fair price. Who knew that there was an entire profession devoted to connecting homeowners and fence builders?

Entrepreneurs recognize that their best opportunities involve offering a unique service that their customers value. That means thinking creatively and regularly trying new approaches. For example, a Colorado hog farmer became concerned about declining sales, so he paid for a simple Google Ad, offering whole pigs for pig roasts. (Hey, they have to come from somewhere!) He was contacted by a chef in a Los Angeles restaurant who was willing to pay top price for a reliable source of dressed pigs, and the hog farmer now has an entirely new market.

What do entrepreneurs who aren't fence brokers or hog farmers look like? They could be:

- Therapists
- Tax preparers
- Office organizers

- Graphic designers
- Writers and editors
- Massage therapists
- Architects
- Eldercare consultants
- Business consultants/analysts
- Web and app developers
- Bookkeepers
- Virtual assistants
- Photographers
- Researchers
- Artists and musicians
- Contractors
- Home repair/handyman/handy ma'am
- Personal chef
- You?

Right now, you may find yourself unexpectedly under- or unemployed. Maybe you're tired of your job and want to strike out on your own. Or perhaps you're already self-employed and are struggling with the business aspect of being your own boss. Being a successful entrepreneur doesn't necessarily mean you need an M.B.A., a fancy office, or venture capital. It does require a vision of how big you can let yourself feel and a commitment to doing what you need to do to bring your vision into the world. This book will help you turn that vision into a thriving business that you find personally and financially rewarding.

There are as many reasons for starting a business as there are entrepreneurs. Some people find themselves without a job and want to see if they can make a living as a freelancer, doing the same type of work for a number of clients instead of for one employer. Others want to find a way to get paid to do what they love. And there are some people who love their jobs but hate dealing with all the energy-draining "overhead" that comes with working within an organization—staff meetings, performance evaluations, office politics, and managing both the boss and staff.

If you are launching "Company You" because you want to get rich quick, prepare to be disappointed. Yes, some entrepreneurs make a million dollars a year—Alan Weiss, author of *The Million-Dollar Consulting,* is a great example of someone who has created a very successful business around what he does best and loves doing. Other entrepreneurs' chief goals are to make enough money to meet their basic living expenses, and much of their "pay" is in the satisfaction they find in their work. Most entrepreneurs, regardless of their income goals, start without an established client base and build their business from an income of $0. It takes most people at least a year to figure out who their *actual* clients are, as opposed to the clients they anticipated, and how to effectively talk about and market their services or products to those clients.

Being an entrepreneur gives you freedom you do not have as an employee:

- You can choose who you work for.
- You can do the kind of work you love.
- You can change your business whenever you want.
- You can work during the hours that work best for you.
- You can probably work from home.
- Your clients come to you because they love what you do.

With this freedom come some downsides that most employees do not experience:

- You won't have a steady paycheck.
- You don't get paid vacation time or sick leave.
- You have to have good client-relationship skills.
- You'll always be marketing your business.
- You don't have co-workers to brainstorm with.

One of the chief benefits of being an entrepreneur is that you can create a business that lets you do what you find most fulfilling. You can learn a new skill, try a new approach, go into an entirely new area, all without a boss telling you that this wasn't what you were hired to do. Are your most productive hours from 11:00 P.M. to 2:00 A.M.? Or starting at 4:00 A.M.? You can build your business around clients who do not need you to be available from 9:00 A.M. to 5:00 P.M. And your office can fully reflect your personality—no more fabric cubicles, and you can forget the no-pets policy.

There is some mental "overhead" that comes with having a business, too. Your income isn't assured, and inevitably there are times when your cash runs low. Both your client base and what you do will probably change over time; the services that people value today may not be the ones they want to pay for in five years. Unless you're starting a business with a partner, you're the only one responsible for getting everything done—marketing, accounting, managing clients, more marketing, and actually doing what your clients pay you for. You can't blame the accounting office for a late invoice, and you can't blame the sales staff when income is slow.

There will be days when you wonder why you started a business, when the downsides feel overwhelming and you're not seeing many upsides to giving up that salary. When I have those days, I remind myself that I always have options. I can shift my thinking about what I do and for whom, and I can wonder about other ways I can have more fun and make a living. I also have the choice to just shut down my business for the afternoon and start fresh the next day; there is no time clock to punch, and I will feel more creative in the morning.

What Makes You Unique?

One characteristic of people who have thrived as entrepreneurs is that they recognize and accept the unique skills, talent, and experience they bring to each client and each project. They learn to look for clients who value and appreciate what they bring to the world, who pay them well and refer them to others in glowing terms. Their primary goal is to create opportunities to do what they do best and to get paid well to do it.

The saying, "Love what you do and you'll never work a day in your life," is not entirely true, but it comes pretty close. I love what I do, and everyone who knows me laughs at the thought of my retiring any time soon; I am enjoying myself too much to want to quit. Sure, there are times when my schedule gets over-full and I'm stretched thin. At the end of one of those days, I always remind myself that I can take tomorrow off and go for a hike; that I voluntarily took this project on because it felt like fun; that *I* get to decide how I spend my days, even the hectic ones. Likewise, there are times when the phone doesn't ring and it feels like all my clients have disappeared. After I take a deep breath, I can sit back and think about where my gifts really lie and how I can express my passion in new ways. I ask myself how I can challenge myself, how I can learn from my clients what they value the most, and how I can start having more fun again.

Your market may be much larger than you think, and you can offer something no one else can.

If you're not sure what your unique gifts are, think back to the last few times you were so engrossed in something that you lost track of time. What were you doing? Were you writing? Leading a group of people? Creating order from chaos? Helping someone plan a move across the country?

Now imagine other contexts in which you could be doing that wonderfully rewarding activity. Right now, part of your job may involve organizing events. How many other kinds of situations need your unique talent in creating successful meetings? Back when I was a librarian in a corporation, I realized that I loved to do research and I was terrible at managing people. So I asked myself how else I could get paid to do what I loved to do and avoid ever managing anyone other than myself. I decided that my best option was to work for myself and to provide research services to business clients. In essence, I built a business centered on finding people to pay me to do what I love to do.

How passionate are you about your star qualities—that unique blend of you that you are bringing to the world? Do you see yourself as one of only a few doing what you do, or are you one of many? As a Colorado hog farmer knows, your market may be much larger than you think, and you may be offering something no one else can offer. Once you recognize that, you'll start seeing more opportunities to find clients who are delighted that they know you.

While some professions tend to require that you and your client are nearby—an office organizer can't tackle my office from a distance, nor can massages be done remotely—consider whether you can provide a service to clients who aren't nearby. My wife is a therapist and life coach who has clients around the world, some of whom she's never met in person. She consults with them on Skype video, even conferencing in other family members when needed. The following questions will help you think of ways that you could provide your service to clients outside your local area.

- Do you provide a tangible product to your clients?
  If so, is it necessary that you be geographically near your

client? Remember, even hog farmers can sell to restaurants in other states.

- Do you provide a professional service to your clients? If so, do you need to be physically face to face with your client? Can you talk over the phone or by Skype or FaceTime?
- Are you focusing on your local market just because that's where you live?

Are there ways you could market yourself and your business virtually (and, thus, to a much broader audience) instead of face to face?

And if you wonder how you can market yourself to people you won't be meeting face to face, check out Chapter 10, *Brand "You."*

How Well Do You Know Yourself?

Working for yourself means that you never get a job performance review again. It also means that you are responsible for assessing your skills, your passions, your fears, and your liabilities. Some of the characteristics of people who have businesses they love include:

- High tolerance for ambiguity
  You'll never have 100 percent of the information you need to have in order to make a decision, take an action, or move in a new direction. As an entrepreneur, you learn how to make choices at the "last best moment"—gathering as much information as is practical until it's time to make a decision—and then making the best choice given what you know at the time.
- Self-motivated and optimistic
  What gets you up in the morning? Do you dread going to work? Entrepreneurs look forward to work because they are consciously creating a business that reflects who they are

and that gives them satisfaction. As an entrepreneur, you recognize setbacks and unpleasant surprises for what they are—an opportunity to find a better, more easeful way of accomplishing your goals. Your default assumption is that you'll find a way to resolve any problem you encounter.

- Willing to work hard for what they want
Creating a business that you love can be a lot of fun; it also requires that you put in the hours required to get everything done. Even when you don't have any clients, you're still working every day, taking all the steps needed to get your business going. You figure out how to use new tools and build new skills that help you build your business.

> *Entrepreneurs make choices at the "last best moment," making the best choice given what they know at the time.*

One of the most rewarding aspects of being an entrepreneur is developing a deep understanding of yourself and of your strengths and talents as well as the habits and routines that may no longer serve you. Here are some of the questions I often ask people who are considering self-employment. There are no right answers; use these questions to see how comfortable you are with the kind of self-reflection useful for entrepreneurs.

- How do you handle stress?
Do you have healthy outlets such as physical activity, a relaxing hobby, or a friend you can call, or do you become unpleasant to those around you?
- How large is your comfort zone?
How do you react when you see that the next step requires you to do something you've never done before and that you aren't confident about?

- What is your history of following through on ideas? Do you have lots of great inspirations that never get beyond the drawing board? Can you recognize an opportunity and initiate action? Do you get discouraged when you don't see immediate results?
- Do you like having a lot of different responsibilities? Will you take on all the roles of a business—marketing manager, CEO, accounts payable clerk, sales director, and IT department, as well as the person who actually does the work?
- Is your life situation such that your household can handle a drop in income while you focus on your business? If this will be a part-time business while you hold down a regular job, do you have the time required for building and marketing the business?
- What are your key nonmonetary rewards from your business? In addition to the profit from your business, how else will you "pay" yourself? A more flexible schedule to accommodate child- or eldercare? The opportunity to travel? A sense of accomplishment? Can you build these rewards into your business so that you're getting "paid" regularly, even when there isn't much revenue?
- Do you thrive being around people, or are you happy to work by yourself? Everyone has both an internal extravert and introvert, and it's important to identify what energizes you. If you really enjoy interacting with others, you'll need to find ways to build that into your business—by joining local networking groups, cultivating local clients and colleagues, and finding volunteer opportunities that connect you with others. If you prefer solitude, you may need to develop your tolerance for

those one-on-one conversations; every business requires some live interaction with prospective clients.

When Will You Start?

For several years before I started my business, I would complain regularly to my sister about how much I hated my job and wanted to start a business. One day, she got tired of hearing me grousing and asked directly, "So, Mary Ellen, when's your launch date?" Gulp. Wanting to sound self-assured, I answered confidently, "In two months." When I hung up the phone, I realized that my launch date would be April 1, which seemed auspicious; every year on April Fool's Day, I would be reminded not to take my business too seriously.

Many now-thriving businesses were started by people who became entrepreneurs out of necessity rather than desire. Finding themselves unemployed and facing a daunting job market, they decided that starting a business might be possible. If you're in this situation, consider whether—deep down in your heart—you really see entrepreneurship as just a way to tide you over until you have another full-time job. Creating a sustainable business takes time, and many of the marketing techniques that are most successful take weeks or months to be effective. If you expect to be working as an employee eventually, you may want to focus your energy on the networking and personal branding aspects of marketing, as these are most likely to get you in front of your potential employers as well as clients.

Whatever kind of entrepreneur you are, at some point you'll make the transition to business owner. Read through Chapter 5, *Building the Framework*, for the basics that should be done before launching your business and then set a date for when you'll begin seeing yourself as an entrepreneur. A countdown to Day Zero can be a powerful incentive to taking the steps you need in order to launch your business.

Five Signs That You're a Reluctant Entrepreneur

- You love what you do, and people seek you out for your expertise.
- The phrases "performance review" and "venture capital" are equally unappealing to you.
- You're comfortable taking action and making decisions.
- You're open to new ideas, and "Yeah, but" isn't in your vocabulary.
- You have a high tolerance for ambiguity.

2 The Joys and Frustrations of Being an Entrepreneur

> "The rule is, jam to-morrow and jam yesterday
> —but never jam to-day."
> "It must come sometimes to 'jam to-day,'" Alice objected.
> "No, it can't," said the Queen. "It's jam every other day:
> to-day isn't any other day, you know."
>
> LEWIS CARROLL, FROM *ALICE'S ADVENTURES IN WONDERLAND*

Starting your own business may be one of the scariest things you've ever done. If you're presently employed, you may be giving up the security of a paycheck—although entrepreneurs would question the security of anyone's job. Your job may include paid vacation and sick leave, health insurance, support for professional development, and other benefits of being an employee. You're now going to become the boss, as well as the office assistant, marketing manager, IT support, and—let's face it—Chief Everything Officer.

If you're going to take the risks required to strike out on your own, you need some tangible rewards as well. Depending on how much face-to-face contact you have with your clients, you have the freedom to work in your PJ's, play polka tunes all day, and go on an afternoon bike ride. Of course, that bike ride may mean that you work late that night, and that is the point. Unlike employees who are confined to a desk, or at least a time clock, you can create a work rhythm that suits you best—one that enables you to make a living doing what you love and live your life easefully.

You may find that you actually enjoy doing things that initially sounded intimidating or downright impossible.

As you read this chapter, think about how important each of these aspects of the business is to you. Some of the downsides almost everyone experiences are the lack of a steady paycheck and the ongoing need to market yourself and your business. Likewise, some features of the entrepreneurial life almost everyone finds rewarding are the flexibility of where we work, the relationships we establish with clients, and the personal satisfaction of knowing that we have built a business ourselves. If you read this chapter and think, "Wow, that sounds like so much more fun than what I'm doing now!" that is a good sign that you're an entrepreneur, reluctant or not.

As you read about the thrills and spills of entrepreneurship, also pay attention to when your stomach clenches up in knots. What aspects sound most challenging to you? Can you imagine yourself being (or becoming) the kind of person who could handle those challenges? Do you see your life continuing to unfold in new and interesting ways, or do you crave a lot of continuity and stability in your life? As long as you're comfortable with the notion of constant, organic evolution, then you will be able to find opportunities to address the challenges of a business. You will recognize new ways to accomplish what you need in a manner that reflects who you really are. And you may surprise yourself by finding that you actually enjoy doing things that initially sounded intimidating or downright impossible.

Keep in mind that very few entrepreneurs started their businesses because they relished the idea of marketing and making collection calls. You can tell a good entrepreneur not by what innate skills and abilities she has but by whether she is willing and able to build the skills she needs. When I started, I had no idea how to plan for quarterly tax payments, for example, and it took me a year to establish a good system for managing my cash flow. It can be challenging to be responsible for recognizing my weaknesses, and one of the most fulfilling aspects of being self-employed is that I have a world of opportunities to build new strengths.

For some of the resources that I have found particularly useful as an entrepreneur, check out Appendix A: Resources for Entrepreneurs and Appendix B: Recommended Books for Reluctant Entrepreneurs.

The Joys of Being an Entrepreneur

Ask a dozen entrepreneurs what they love the most about how they make a living, and you will get at least two dozen answers. What is rewarding now may not have been what motivated them at the beginning of their businesses, but entrepreneurs always find nonmonetary ways by which they regularly "pay" themselves. Here are some of the aspects of self-employment that most of us find particularly rewarding.

- Set your own hours.
  Having a customizable schedule means that you can incorporate the rest of your life into your day. You can arrange your hours around your child's school schedule, a doctor's appointment, the plumber, and lunch with a friend.

In fact, a colleague of mine raised four kids, including twin boys, while working from home. Once the children were settled in preschool or with Dad or a babysitter, she closed her office door and told her family they could interrupt her only if disaster hit. She often started work at 5:00 A.M., which enabled her to end her work day in time to meet her kids when they came home from school.

- Take pride in ownership.

There is a certain pride of ownership that comes with being an entrepreneur. I know that my clients could use someone else for business analysis; they come to me because they know and trust me, and they are confident that I will be able to help them. I feel a great deal of satisfaction knowing that I can create an income doing what I love doing.

- Reinvent yourself.

We entrepreneurs can reinvent ourselves every six months if we want to. Since we are talking directly with our clients, we know what they want and value, and we can shift in response to their changing needs. No need to consult with the boss or the boss's boss or run it by three feasibility committees. If it sounds like fun and passes the straight-face test for feasibility, we try it.

- Dream big.

We can have absurdly big dreams and make the choices to bring those dreams to life. Entrepreneurs tend to see the glass as half full; we see that our business has unlimited possibilities. Our businesses are a way to manifest more fun in our lives as well as a way to make a living, so we assume that there will always be a joyful way to accomplish anything that needs to be done.

- Be part of a network.

We can create a network of support around us, and who doesn't need some support? We find mentors, we create mastermind groups, we consult with colleagues, we even enlist our friends and loved ones as cheerleaders. There are also professional associations for everything from acne researchers to zoologists; see if there is an association for your professional interests. If you don't already know of an association of people just like you, check out the Gateway to Associations, described in more detail in Appendix A: Resources for Entrepreneurs.

- Develop life skills.
  We develop life skills that enable us to feel comfortable with uncertainty, take strategic risks, operate rationally when we are afraid, listen to our gut, and trust ourselves. We learn how to accept responsibility, not blame, and how to maintain a constant state of curiosity. We build the skills to listen without filters, think creatively, and assume that there is a solution for any problem.

- Love your boss!
  You don't hear most employees saying how much they enjoy their job, their co-workers, or their boss. The self-employed, on the other hand, have a good working relationship with their boss, whom they see in the mirror every morning. While I jokingly complain about how much my boss makes me work sometimes, she also has a casual dress code and lets me bring my dogs to the office.

- "Think outside the box" — what box?
  One of the most frustrating aspects of working in a traditional job, at least for me, was the bureaucracy that inevitably slowed down innovation and change. If I wanted to develop a new initiative, it required meetings, proposals, focus groups, and approvals. A certain amount of structural inertia is built into almost any organization. While that provides stability, it also means that change takes time. As a one- or two-person business, you can change your approach

whenever it is needed. Want to offer a new service to your clients? Expand into a new area? Start a blog? Refocus your marketing to a different client base? No problem! You can be fearless in your approach because you know that you can regroup if you see that something does not work as you had expected.

- Increase your job satisfaction.

   An entrepreneur does not get an annual review (or pay raise) from the boss, and the lack of formal feedback and reinforcement can be difficult for some people. On the other hand, you can find a lot of satisfaction in knowing that your clients keep coming back to you because they really like what you do and they are willing to pay you to do it. A related benefit is the supportive note that comes when you least expect it. As I was writing this chapter, I received a message from someone who follows me in the social media, telling me how much she appreciates a webinar I created and how grateful she is that I took the time to do it. That kind of response makes my day. I believe that entrepreneurs hear more genuine thank-yous than traditional employees do; our clients are far more aware of what value we bring to them than employers are, since our clients are directly paying for that value.

- Choose who you work with.

   One of the less-tangible benefits of running your own business is the ability to turn down projects or clients you just don't want to work with—within reason, of course. Sooner or later, everyone runs into the Client from Hell, someone who makes unreasonable demands, is consistently rude or abrasive, or represents an organization or cause with which, for whatever reason, you would rather not work. Since you're running the show, you can decide that you simply won't do business with that person. By the same token, you can decide to discount your rate or donate your services to a nonprofit or charitable organization that you do support. Being able to incorporate your personal values into your business can be a gratifying aspect of entrepreneurship. For more discussion on establishing and maintaining good relationships with your clients, see Chapter 8, *The Care and Feeding of Clients.*

No Regrets

Bronnie Ware worked for years as a palliative-care nurse and had the opportunity to be with many people during the last few weeks of their lives. During her conversations with patients, she often asked whether they had any regrets or would have done anything differently. The most common five that she heard were these:

- I wish I'd had the courage to live a life true to myself, not the life others expected of me.
- I wish I hadn't worked so hard. ("This came from every male patient that I nursed," she noted.)
- I wish I'd had the courage to express my feelings.
- I wish I had stayed in touch with my friends.
- I wish that I had let myself be happier.

As I read through this list, I am struck by how fortunate entrepreneurs are. We can live a life true to ourselves. We can integrate our work and home lives. We can strengthen our ties to our community of friends. We can be clear in all of our interactions. And we can choose to create a business that brings us happiness. How much easier all that is when we are free to create a living that truly reflects our passions!

To read more about each of the above regrets, go to

www.inspirationandchai.com/Regrets-of-the-Dying.html

For more on Ware's observations, see her memoir, The Top Five Regrets of the Dying: A Life Transformed by the Dearly Departing.

The Frustrations of Being an Entrepreneur

Now that you have an appreciation of the benefits—both tangible and intangible—of being an entrepreneur, it is time to look at the not-so-glamorous aspects of being your own boss. Take a deep breath as you read through this list, keeping in mind that for every challenge there is a solution—or at least a satisfactory accommodation.

- Scheduling work hours to meet the needs of your client
Regardless of their niche, most entrepreneurs tell me that they regularly work six days a week. We all need to be available during the hours convenient to our clients, which is often not only 9:00 A.M. to 5:00 P.M., Monday through Friday. Most people whose business involves face-to-face interactions—therapists, for example—need to be available both during the week and on Saturday.

- Always marketing yourself
You're always marketing yourself, although it does not have to feel like marketing. No entrepreneur has a guaranteed pool of clients, and no client lasts forever. Even after you've been in business for years, you're still marketing; your business will evolve and you'll always be talking with prospective clients. For some people, this is the most difficult part of running a business: "How can I tell people how great I am without sounding conceited or pompous?" Chapter 9, *Your (Fabulous) Marketing Plan*, goes into marketing issues in depth; the short answer here is that being an entrepreneur means learning to look at yourself as a brand, a product, a business. Even after you've been in business for five or ten years, you still need to market yourself, although the amount of time you spend on marketing will drop significantly as you become more established in your field.

- Thinking of yourself as a business
  You have to think of yourself as a business. You have to figure out what other people want, value, and will pay you to do. That means shifting your thinking from that of an employee or freelancer to that of a business owner, which for many people can be challenging. For example, it's easy to let the first few contacts you make determine the direction of your business. Just because your tennis partner likes your idea does not ensure that you have a sustainable business model. Instead, you need to think strategically about your unique set of skills and passions, your market, and your vision for your business in order to be offering something your clients value.

- Building business skills
  You need business skills like keeping track of client invoices and payments, managing unhappy clients, collecting from past-due clients, negotiating with clients and vendors, and managing your cash flow. If you feel that you're weak in one of these areas, focus on developing your skills by taking a professional development or continuing education course, reading up on the subject, or working with a coach. For example, one area that many of us find challenging is how to effectively market. Chapter 9, *Your (Fabulous) Marketing Plan*, and Chapter 10, *Brand "You,"* give you a number of ideas on how to promote yourself and your business in ways that feel authentic and genuine. Also see "With a Little Help from My Friends" below for a list of what can and cannot be easily delegated to someone outside your business. You can build business skills with the tools in Chapter 7, *All About Money*, and in Chapter 8, *The Care and Feeding of Clients*.

- Creating a business from scratch
  You have to create your business from scratch. You must decide what kind of business you want, and that means deciding everything from whether to incorporate to what your pricing structure is, what your web site will say about you, and what your clients will look like. Every decision is yours to make, and you have to be willing to make decisions quickly, often without all the information you'd like to have.
- Motivating yourself
  You have to motivate yourself. No one else will get you out of bed, into your office, and working every morning. No one notices when you spend the day looking at videos of cats doing silly things. No one congratulates you when you finish a difficult project, and no one encourages you when you lose a big client. You decide when you need to take a break or when you need to buckle down and work like crazy. Of course, this can be one of the benefits of being an entrepreneur, too. Chapter 6, *Managing Yourself and Your Business*, gives you some tools for being your own manager. And you can create a support network of friends, family, and colleagues who will give you a boost of energy when you need it.
- Managing your time
  Time management is critical, particularly during your first year of business. You could face a week—or five—with no work coming in. You could surprise yourself by how many ways you can procrastinate or goof off when you don't have looming deadlines. You'll learn to look at "free" time differently as a business owner—any hour not spent doing paying work can be spent generating paying work. Even if you don't like structured time, you need to learn how to make the best use of the hours that you work. For me, that might mean doing my writing early in the morning when I

feel most creative and saving my time on social media for whenever I have a free fifteen or twenty minutes during the day.

- "Where did my money go?"
  Two of the challenges that almost every entrepreneur faces are cash flow and pricing. Even after many years in business, you'll probably find that some months you're flush with cash and some months you're running low—usually, it seems, just before you have to pay your taxes. Besides the obvious need to put aside surplus income in anticipation of the lean times, it takes a strong stomach to ride out those periods when you've sent invoices out but none of the checks have come in.

- Putting a value on your time
  Pricing your services is the other financial-related aspect of the business that many entrepreneurs find difficult. Quoting an estimate for a project can be hard, particularly when you have no idea what your competitors are charging or offering. In general, beginning entrepreneurs tend to undercharge relative to what clients pay for other professional services. Knowing how much to charge, accurately estimating what the market will bear, and setting a price that appropriately reflects the expertise and value we offer is difficult for many of us. I address the challenges of pricing in more detail in Chapter 7, *All About Money*.

- Vacation? What Vacation?
  Vacations pose problems for entrepreneurs. For starters, there's no such thing as a paid vacation for the self-employed. (That's not quite true; I will sometimes arrive early on a business trip so that I can play tourist for a day or two, but I don't count that as a vacation.) Part of the reason we entrepreneurs learn to price ourselves at the high end of the scale is that our income has to cover the time we take

off. A related challenge is what you do with your clients while you are away. That's what mobile phones are for, you say. Sure, you can monitor your e-mail and voicemail while you are relaxing on the beach. But is that any way to enjoy your vacation? One of the things I value the most about a vacation is being able to leave my job behind, which is why vacations to locations with spotty Internet access are so appealing. See Chapter 6, *Managing Yourself and Your Business*, for more thoughts on keeping your business going while you get away from it all. In addition to vacations, there is the inevitable doctor appointment, time spent taking your car in to get fixed, and cleanup when the dog encounters a skunk—again. Employees are usually paid for a certain amount of personal time off; we entrepreneurs don't have that option. Generally, if we're not working, we're not earning.

With a Little Help from My Friends
You're great at what you do; fortunately, you don't have to be great at all aspects of running a business. Some tasks can be contracted out fairly easily while others are more difficult to delegate.

Easy to contract out:

- Accounting
- Collections
- Design and writing of marketing material
- Web site design
- Scheduling
- Computer maintenance and purchasing

Plenty of other entrepreneurs and small businesses offer these services, which means that you can probably find an affordable professional to handle your needs.

Not as easy to contract out:

- Strategic planning
- Client contact
- Estimating cost and time for projects
- Being the face of your business

All of these require a full understanding of who you are, what you do, and what you dream of doing. Note that I did not include marketing in either list. Entrepreneurs who offer a highly personalized service need to be able to market themselves; their clients are buying a specific person. However, if you are selling a product or service that is fairly straightforward, you may be able to contract out some marketing tasks. See Chapter 9, Your (Fabulous) Marketing Plan, *for ideas on how to share the word about your business without becoming a walking, talking billboard.*

As you consider both the positive and negative aspects of being an entrepreneur, remember that your comfort level will expand as your business grows. Things that seem intimidating or even distasteful now—marketing, talking about your fees, managing a business—become easier over time, and you'll find ways to build the business that you enjoy and that reflects who you really are.

The Best and Worst of Being an Entrepreneur
Before you launch your own business, think about whether the "bests" outweigh the "worsts."

Best:

- Satisfaction in doing what you love and being paid for it
- Pride of ownership; taking credit for the success of your business
- Flexibility about where, when, and how you work
- Meeting and developing relationships with a wide variety of clients and colleagues
- Freedom from bureaucracy

Worst:

- Stress of ownership; being responsible for the success of your business
- Being available whenever your clients need you
- Cash flow fluctuations

Five Key Attributes of a Reluctant Entrepreneur

- You can feel scared and still take action.
- You can keep yourself motivated.
- You know you have a valuable set of skills.
- You believe that you can create a business you enjoy.
- You are optimistic, and you assume that you'll find a way to accomplish your goals.

3 The Mind of an Entrepreneur

> "There's no use trying," [Alice] said:
> "one ca'n't believe impossible things."
> "I daresay you haven't had much practice," said the Queen.
> "When I was your age, I always did it for half-an-hour a day.
> Why, sometimes I've believed as many as six impossible things
> before breakfast."
>
> LEWIS CARROLL, FROM *THROUGH THE LOOKING-GLASS*

For many of us reluctant entrepreneurs, the hardest step is just seeing ourselves as business owners. I can hear you now: "Yikes—I want to do what I love, not look at a profit and loss statement— whatever that is." Making the shift from thinking like an employee to thinking like an entrepreneur can feel strange and awkward. Most of us are accustomed to interacting within larger organizations—in school, at work, in faith communities—where roles are distributed among a number of people. You choose among a range of responsibilities, including simply that of participant.

We self-employed people wear all the hats of the organization, all the time. Over the course of a day, I may be thinking like a marketing professional while I contact a conference organizer about a speaking opportunity; a salesperson when someone who reads my blog calls me to inquire about a coaching package; a bookkeeper as I pay bills and monitor cash flow; and strategic planner when I sit down to plan my week's activities.

Build a Better Mousetrap

You may have a great idea for a new business, and you know that you would buy the product yourself, so you figure that it must be a good idea.

> *The first step in learning to think like an entrepreneur is to recognize that you probably don't know as much as you think you know.*

I'm not sure if there was ever a time when, if you built a better mousetrap and just sat there, people would beat a path to your door. These days, "merely" developing a great product or service is no longer enough. You may have learned this yourself. Have you ever developed a workshop that you thought would be well-received, put out flyers and advertised in all the right places, and had to cancel because no one registered? Have you wondered why some people's workshops are filled to capacity and others' are sparsely attended?

People buy from people they know—or at least know about. That's why the local assisted-living facility offers free workshops for caregivers, so that when your own parent becomes unable to live independently, you already have a good impression of their operation and staff. It's one reason why Boulder therapist Julie Colwell offers free and low-cost events virtually every week. Through her fishbowl coaching sessions and meetings on the basics of conscious living, people get to know her and are inclined to attend her weekend workshops, join her learning group, and buy her books.

It's easy to make assumptions about who your potential clients are and what products or services you'll offer. Just because you think that your handmade paisley and polka-dot tea cozies are adorable doesn't mean that there's a market for them. Your customers may not think like you; in fact, they may want what you offer precisely because they value your unique approach to their problem. For example, when I'm looking for a fitness coach, I want someone who knows how to motivate a coach potato, not someone who assumes I look forward to a strenuous workout at 6:00 A.M.

Before you start your business, step back and assume that you don't know what your customers want the most. You probably have some hunches, and your friends all assure you that there'll be a huge market for what you offer. But until you hear that positive feedback from people who are prepared to pay you, you haven't yet gotten input from the people who matter the most—your clients. Seek feedback from potential customers through one-on-one conversations, surveys, focus groups, social media, and any other means that reach your audience. Ask them what they value the most with respect to your product or service. Depending on your market, you might ask questions like these:

- What do you value most in a marketing consultant? Can you describe a great experience you had?
- How did you learn about your massage therapist? Personal referral? An ad? An event?
- What do you do when you aren't getting enough business from your web site?
- What would you be able to do that you can't do now if you had a virtual assistant?

- If you were buying this type of art, what would you expect to pay? What would make you buy it?
- Do you see your accountant as a part of your strategic team? Could you use a more consultative accountant?

The Imposter Syndrome
"Hi. I'm Mary Ellen and I'm faking it."

No, I'm not going to put that on a conference name badge, but if I did, I know a lot of people would sidle up to me and admit that they, too, are faking it. We're the people who, at one time or another, suffer from what is known as the Imposter Syndrome. Do you worry that people will finally realize that you're not the smart, capable expert they once thought you were? Do you think that your success is due to luck or a fluke rather than because you are an astute business owner? Do you obsess about making a mistake and interpret any constructive criticism as further proof of your incompetence?

Many of us suffer from this fear of someone finally discovering that we have no particular skills or abilities—that what we're doing is so easy that anyone could do it. In fact, what often causes the Imposter Syndrome is our undervaluing of our own innate talents and gifts. If something comes naturally to us, we assume that it must be easy for everyone and that we would look foolish for bragging about it.

The people most likely to experience the Imposter Syndrome often seem to be high achievers, those labeled as "gifted" as children, and those who have very specialized skills. From my own experience, it appears that a lot of reluctant entrepreneurs fit that profile. In fact, one of the appeals of being our own boss is that we don't have to worry about co-workers finally discovering that we're the frauds we believe we really are.

These feelings of self-doubt and inadequacy may never disappear entirely, but you can learn to recognize them when they show up and counteract them. Here are a few techniques that can help.

- Avoid using words like "only" or "just" when describing or thinking about your expertise and background.
- Don't apologize for yourself or insult yourself. Don't attribute to luck what you created yourself by recognizing an opportunity.
- Trust your clients' judgment. Are you truly surrounded by such foolish people that no one sees the true you? Perhaps it's more likely that their evaluation of you is as accurate as their evaluation of others.
- Give yourself a pep talk. Say things like, "I love taking on a challenge" or "I know I can figure this out as I go along" or "It will get easier each time I do this."

Being Your Own Manager

One of the responsibilities I don't miss from my days as a manager is writing annual job performance reviews. I never felt like "exceeds expectations" adequately expressed my appreciation for an employee's initiative, and I always hated the discussions about performance that "needs improvement." However, I found it challenging when I left my last paycheck job to learn the discernment required to know whose advice to take to heart and whose to treat more lightly.

When I announced to everyone I knew that I had launched my business, I received lots of advice from business colleagues, especially those with a marketing or strategic planning background: start a cold-call program; write a business plan and get funding; hire a marketer; develop a niche; develop a broad clientele base; charge by the hour; never charge by the hour. It all sounded so reasonable, even when it was contradictory.

I have learned over time that all advice and input is useful, even when it isn't directly relevant to my current situation and even when it isn't what I want to hear. One of my clients called me at the end of a project to complain about the report I had sent. The format wasn't right, it didn't have the sections she wanted, and it was too densely written. After my initial wave of nausea and the desire to crawl under a rock, I realized that she had higher expectations of me than I had of myself. She was going to present the report to the executive director of her organization, and she trusted that I could prepare something that would reflect well on her. After I sent her the final, polished report and was able to look back dispassionately on the experience, I saw that my lesson was to start seeing myself as my client's partner, not just a "vendor." It's my responsibility to look at my client's end result and to figure out my role in getting her to her goal.

> *The most effective way to battle your what-ifs is to simply act like the confident, competent person that you would like to be seen as.*

Stepping up to a higher level of performance is scary. What if you blow it? What if you find yourself tongue-tied in front of a microphone? What if you embarrass yourself in front of others? What if your client doesn't like your new product or service? And aren't there other people who are much better at what they do than you are? My answer to all these questions is, "Oh well." You've undoubtedly failed at something in your life and you survived. You've been speechless and eventually found your voice. You've been embarrassed and gotten over it. Not everyone will like what you offer. And though everyone is more skilled at something than you are, you bring a unique set of skills, passion, and expertise to every client.

The most effective way to battle all these what-ifs is to simply act like the confident, competent person that you would like to be seen as. Yes, one way of saying that is, "Fake it 'til you make it," but that feels inauthentic and dishonest to many people. However, you can also see this as an opportunity to learn how to show the authentic you—bringing out in the open your enthusiasm, love of what you do, and commitment to your clients. This is an acquired skill and one that creates a wonderful self-perpetuating cycle. As you convey to your clients your confidence that you're offering them something valuable, they begin to reflect that confidence back to you.

Freelancer or Business Owner?

For most people, the shift from employee mindset to entrepreneur vision comes gradually as they become more and more comfortable with looking at themselves more strategically. (Did you just flinch at the word "strategically"? Take a deep breath. Exhale. It's easier than it feels right now.)

If most of your work experience has been as an employee, you're probably familiar with being involved in ongoing processes. Even if you work on specific projects, those are all done within the context of the continuing activities of your organization. As an entrepreneur, on the other hand, you're usually engaged to accomplish something rather than simply become part of a process. This is a distinction that new businesspeople often miss; your clients won't pay you for what you did in your last job as an employee, even if it was in a related field. They'll pay you to solve a specific problem or meet a specific need that they can't get within their organization.

One way to help shift your mindset is to look at your language. Do you call yourself a freelancer, self-employed, or a consultant or business owner? The word you use will suggest to other people how you see yourself, and the more customized and individualized your focus, the more valuable you're seen by your clients. This doesn't always mean you have to develop additional skills to become more valuable; you just change your relationship with your clients from that of an order-taker to a peer.

- Freelancers see themselves as a set of hired hands, handling the overflow work or filling in for someone else. Their value is in being a substitute for a full-time employee.
- Self-employed people see themselves as a one-person business, looking for ways they can help their clients.
- Consultants and business owners view themselves as partners with their clients and focus on learning what their clients' critical needs are and exploring ways to help their clients achieve their goals.

Your success is tied to how you see yourself in relation to your clients. The more focused you are on the client's outcome—what happens after the project is done or the product is delivered—the more your clients value you. And clients who value you are happy to pay your professional fees. Everyone wins: your client's problem is solved, you get paid well, and you know that you've made a difference with your client.

> *Your clients don't pay you for what you did in your last job as an employee. They pay you to solve a specific problem or meet a specific need that they can't get within their organization.*

For example, someone who sees himself as a self-employed transcriptionist describes his business as listening to a recording, typing up what he hears, and sending it to his client. If, on the other hand, he finds out that the transcription will be used as the basis of a speech and creates the transcript in a specialized format, he's thinking like a consultant. He identifies a need and works with his client to find out how he can make his work more useful to his client and more directly targeted to his client's need.

Successful entrepreneurs share. An accountant who knows that she needs to build trust with her clients provides plenty of resources on her web site, such as a retirement planning guide, checklist of what to look for in an accountant, financial calculators, and a video of her introducing herself and talking about her commitment to her clients. An accountant who thinks of herself as just a freelancer might be reluctant to include any resources that prospective clients might be able to use themselves, for fear of losing them as paying clients.

Money-Think

When I started my business, one of my challenges was to shift my thinking about money. I set up separate business checking and savings accounts and seeded them with the money I'd saved up to invest in my business. And the key word here is "invest." I learned that I do have to spend money in order to generate revenue; if I don't, I'm probably losing an opportunity to build a stronger business. Every year, I include money in my budget for at least one professional conference—not to market to clients but for my own learning. As a side note, one of the benefits of developing my presentation skills is that I'm invited to speak at (and attend) a wide range of conferences. This serves as a form of professional development because I can listen to the concerns and trends in a wide range of industries and professions.

I also learned early on that I'd have to deal with the inevitable fluctuation of cash flow. Some weeks are going to be crazy-busy, and then I'll go through a stretch of days or weeks when no one calls. During those dry spells, I spend at least twenty hours a week on marketing—blogging, lining up speaking engagements, getting articles published, reaching out to recent clients, and so on.

As I saw how my business fluctuated over the course of a year, I began to relax during the usual dry spells. I knew that August was always going to be slow, so I needed to put money aside during the busy times to tide me over during the dry periods. And I now schedule my vacations around times that I know are going to be slow, which lets me relax about taking a week off without checking my phone and e-mail.

Being an entrepreneur means looking at yourself in a different way. If you try building a business by being the therapist with the lowest rates in town, you'll find that your clientele will leave you for the next therapist who's just starting her practice and pricing herself low. Instead, you can focus on what problem or desire your clients have that you can meet in a way no one else can. Sure, there are lots of financial planners out there, but who else brings your fifteen years of experience working with families with special-needs kids?

Clients pay you based on how much value you provide, not just how much time or effort you put into the job. Make sure that what you finally give your client represents all the value and time you put into it. If you're a photographer, for example, make sure that your prints are framed and displayed in ways that highlight the unique features of your art.

Learning to Love Fear

Here's a secret that every business owner eventually learns. You can be scared speechless and still take action. Feeling afraid is rarely physically immobilizing; it just saps your will and determination. Your body will continue to function if you can simply sit with the fear.

I used to be terrified of speaking in public and of interacting with anyone I hadn't known for at least a decade. I managed to get past the immobilized-by-fear state by reminding myself of the following facts: I am feeling afraid. My body has adrenalin coursing through it. My lizard brain is screaming, "FLEE!" I thank my lizard brain for being so clear.

Now I notice myself just sitting still and breathing. Yes, I can sit still and just breathe.

And here's where the magic happens. I find out that, even as I'm feeling scared, I can walk forward into whatever terrifies me. Moving forward and feeling scared can happen simultaneously. I still have full control over all my appendages.

I go forward into whatever it is that scares me. I go into the room full of people I don't know, and I strike up a conversation with a stranger. I can stand at a podium and know that everyone in the room is my ally.

After enough times, my reptile brain learns that whatever it is that scares me so much actually isn't all that frightening.

Exercising Your Entrepreneurial Muscles

Part of making a living as a one-person business involves stretching yourself all the time. Lots of people have great ideas; what sets you apart is that you take action. Rather than waiting for the perfect time to launch a business, you decide when the timing is good enough. Instead of worrying about achieving perfection, you learn from talking with clients about what they most value, and you provide something as close to that as you can, within the budget and timeframe you've negotiated with your client.

The most valuable asset that you manage is your time. You have only so many hours in the day during which you can work, and you're responsible for managing that time so that your goals are met. Virtually everything you do can tie into something else that you do. If you have an interesting take on a new development in your field of expertise, blog about it, tweet about it, incorporate it into a project you're working on, and think about how to work it into other aspects of your business.

Having the mind of an entrepreneur means always looking at yourself from your client's perspective. How easy is it to find your contact information? How easy is it to get you on the phone? Are you nice to work with or do you have a reputation for being prickly? How clear are you about your prices and services? How confident do you sound? How committed are you to each client's project? Once a year, check in with each of your clients to find out what they value the most right now. Do they still really love or need what you offer, or have you become a nice-to-have? If you've become a nonessential, ask your clients what you could offer that they'd buy. (This is a scary question; you may learn that what you thought was tremendously valuable isn't seen that way by your clients anymore. Be willing to simply take in whatever your clients have to say.)

Listen for feedback from clients about what differentiates you from others. You bring a unique combination of experience, interests, and passion to the table. What else can you do with that one-of-a-kind product? What sets you apart is your brain, your creativity, your focus on your clients. Ask each client, "How could I make this more useful/valuable/better for you? What else could I do for you?"

In addition to listening to your clients, watch for opportunities to look at your business from a fresh perspective. Keep asking yourself, "What next?" As you finish a project, spend time thinking about what you've learned, what new insights you've gained, and how you can apply these lessons to your business.

Recognize how brave you are. You get to create a living that lets you do what you love, in a rhythm and pace that works best for you, because you're willing to push yourself past your comfort zone. You're taking risks, knowing that doing so enables you to live the life you want to live.

Five Mindset Must-Haves

- People buy from people they know—or at least know about. So make sure you're building relationships with as many potential clients as possible.
- Step back and assume that you don't know what your customers want the most.
- Clients pay you to solve a specific problem or meet a specific need that they cannot resolve themselves.
- It's your responsibility to communicate your value, not your clients' responsibility to discern your value for themselves.
- Your business will always be evolving; let go of your attachment to "how it used to be."

4 Who Are Your Clients?

> "I see nobody on the road," said Alice.
> "I only wish I had such eyes," the King remarked in a fretful tone.
> "To be able to see Nobody! And at that distance, too!
> Why, it's as much as I can do to see real people, by this light!"
>
> LEWIS CARROLL, FROM *THROUGH THE LOOKING-GLASS*

Some people start their business by offering something they think people will want. I watched as a chili-and-ice-cream shop (yes, really!) opened near me with high hopes. The owner was passionate about chili and he loved ice cream, so he figured that he'd be so successful that he could franchise his concept within a year. His shop offered five delicious types of chili and four great flavors of ice cream, and though I can attest to the quality of the food, the store didn't last six months. There were only so many times that his customers wanted to eat chili and ice cream, and he couldn't compete with nearby restaurants that offered more varied menus.

A more sustainable business is one that is built around what you love to do *and* what people will happily pay you for. This chapter helps you figure out both parts of the key elements of a successful business—making a living while doing something you enjoy.

What's Your Bliss?

Think back to the last few times you were so engrossed in something that you lost track of time. What were you doing? Leading a group of people? Helping a teenager make sense of life? Photographing dogs in the park? Helping an out-of-town family care for an elderly parent?

Now sit back and imagine the details of what you were doing. What part of that activity was giving you the most enjoyment? Do you particularly enjoy being out in the park with dogs or is it the look on the face of the owner when she sees that you have captured the spirit of her dog in a photo? Would you also enjoy photographing toddlers at the playground or taking studio shots of people and their animals?

> *What you do in your business may not look much like what you did as an employee.*

Say you are a nurse and now you want to work for yourself. Your options might include teaching nurses about communication skills, providing workshops on living with diabetes, coaching clients in healthier lifestyle choices, or supporting legal professionals preparing for a trial.

If you're fluent in Arabic, you could provide intense tutoring for executives doing business in the Middle East. On top of that, if you are familiar with (or can learn) technical terminology for specific industries—engineering, say, or medicine—your value to your clients would be that much greater.

Perhaps you've always been interested in real estate. You go to open houses just to see what the property looks like and to get ideas on home renovation. After training and certification as an appraiser, you could work with real estate agents who need a property appraised and with banks and credit unions evaluating mortgage properties.

Keep in mind that what you do in your business may not look much like what you did as an employee, and there's a reason for that. Employers need people who can do their job within the context of a larger organization. Employees don't have to worry about paying rent for their office space or reminding a big client to pay the last invoice. Employees generally get to focus on doing what they are paid to do, whether that's designing marketing material, caring for patients, or managing a large IT project. As an entrepreneur, you'll be looking not only at what you do but also why people value what you do. What problem, need, or want can you address?

What Is Your Client's Problem?

As you create a business that reflects your passion, imagine what your clients would pay you for if you could offer whatever service or product they really wanted. What do they see as their biggest problem, most pressing need, or their heart's desire? And is this problem going to recur or is it likely to be a one-time need? A researcher I know started a business providing background information for patients recently diagnosed with serious medical conditions. His clients were very grateful—he would develop customized packages of material on alternative treatments, patient support groups, and clinical trials for new drugs. However, he had very few repeat customers (which, of course, is a good thing for his customers!) and he found that this business model required far too much marketing for the income it generated. He shifted his focus to helping hospitals develop their outreach efforts to the community and build awareness of their areas of expertise, which enabled him to touch the lives of even more people while building a sustainable business of repeat customers.

Consider whether your clients need to be nearby or whether they can be anywhere in the world. For some jobs, you may need to meet your clients face to face—chimney sweeps cannot work remotely, and you can't get a massage from someone halfway around the world. However, a quick scan of Elance.com, oDesk.com, and other freelance job sites makes it clear that there are plenty of opportunities to serve your clients regardless of where they're located. My wife, a therapist and life coach, has clients all over the world, many of whom meet with her through Skype video. Some of her calls come early in the morning or late at night; the tradeoff is that her business is stronger because her potential market is worldwide rather than limited to the town where we live.

> *Don't worry if you have a business idea*
> *that not everyone likes. Focus on meeting the needs*
> *of an identifiable group of people.*

Don't worry if you have a business idea that not everyone likes. It's impossible to provide a product or service that everyone wants or needs—or even values. Instead, focus on meeting the needs of an identifiable group of people—helping real estate agents "stage" homes to showcase each house's unique features, serving as a virtual assistant for start-up companies, or designing product packaging and marketing material for the hospitality industry.

The Reality-Check Interviews

Once you have an idea of what product or service you're offering and who would happily pay you, it's time to do a reality check. Keep in mind that you are not your client (remember that chili-and-ice-cream store that only the owner loved). For most people, this is the most challenging aspect of starting a business: learning whether people value what you're offering and want to pay you well for it. The best way to find out is to shut up and listen.

I call these conversations "reality-check interviews." You're interviewing prospective clients to learn about their pain points and what needs you can address, and to find out whether your assumptions are aligned with reality. Although this step may not sound like fun, it's a vital part of creating a business that can sustain you.

Are You My Customer?

First, think about the kind of people you think would be your customers. If you're an event planner, your clients might be marketing professionals and HR departments within organizations, convention and visitors bureaus, and public relations companies. If you're a virtual assistant, your customers could be small-business owners, one-person businesses, and small nonprofits. If your passion is videography, your clients might be production companies.

One of the most effective ways I've found to reach out to people I want to interview is to use the social networking site LinkedIn.com. A basic account is free, and your LinkedIn profile can serve as another place to promote yourself and your services. Use its search feature to find people who meet your criteria for possible clients, and then contact them through LinkedIn and ask for a brief interview. Since the people you contact can immediately look at your profile and learn something about you, they may be more likely to agree to a conversation. Chapter 10, *Brand "You,"* covers how to use social networks for getting your name out.

You'll learn the most if you talk with people who don't know you well. Your friends, family, and colleagues already have assumptions about who you are and what you do, so their answers are often filtered through those assumptions. Instead, reach out to people with whom you have some connection—a friend of a friend who regularly buys products or services similar to what you have in mind, someone you're connected to through LinkedIn or other social networks who you think could be a client, or someone you've met at a conference or networking event who sounded interested in what you do. At the end of each interview, remember to not only thank them for their time and insight but also to ask for names of anyone they know who you could briefly talk with. Strangers are far more likely to respond when you can say, "Robin suggested that I talk with you," and each referral gets you that much farther from your own assumptions and perspective.

These aren't marketing conversations. You're not promoting your business to the people you're talking with; you're asking them questions in order to learn what their biggest concerns are and what they want most. You'll be talking with people who you think represent your potential clients.

When I started my company, I thought I'd provide industry profiles to business marketers who needed to understand their customers. However, after several conversations with marketing professionals, I learned that they didn't see much value in my industry profiles. Rather, they wanted information that answered their deeper questions—what their clients are most concerned about, what their biggest competitors were up to, and what new areas they could expand into. Thanks to my reality-check interviews, I avoided wasting months of time talking to my prospective clients about something they didn't really care about.

What Do You Really Want?

These conversations involve more than simply chatting with someone. Your goal is to be able to look at the world from your clients' perspective. You need to prepare open-ended questions that are clear and that—as much as possible—don't assume anything about your client's situation. Your goal is to learn as much as possible about what motivates your clients to buy products or services similar to what you have in mind. Your questions will, of course, be driven by who you think your clients are. Here are some examples of the kinds of questions that enable you to glean useful information, all designed to elicit your clients' biggest concern or need and to learn how they describe that concern.

- An event planner might ask: What are your goals when you schedule a conference? What would ensure that it's as successful as possible? What do you wish you could do to enhance the value of the event?

- A mobile app developer might ask: Could you describe the last couple of times when you brought in a developer? How did you find him or her? What were your chief concerns? When during your planning process could a developer have been most valuable?

- A photographer might ask: What are the occasions when you would want a photographer? What would you pay to have a professional "head shot" portrait that highlights your personality and character? What about candid photos of you and your pet?

- A business consultant might ask: How do you maintain a competitive edge—both you professionally and your company within the industry? What do you wish you knew about your competition? What keeps you awake at night?

Note that none of these are yes-or-no questions. They're all open-ended and encourage your contacts to think about what they want and value, and they help you learn how your potential customers recognize and describe that need. Your goal, by the end of each of these conversations, is to see the world through your customers' eyes and to describe your value in terms that resonate with your market.

> *You're creating a business around your clients' needs, and that means you have to learn everything you can about their needs before you launch your business.*

During these short interviews—aim for no more than fifteen or twenty minutes—your job is to ask questions and listen to the answers. You aren't talking about the fabulous services you could provide; you are just listening to what the other person is telling you. Ask follow-up questions to learn enough so that you can later design a product or service that your clients will find immediately beneficial.

Once you have had five or six of these conversations, you'll have a better idea of what your market's biggest concerns are and in what situations they would be willing to pay well for what you do. Now consider how you can add even more value to what you do and make your product or service unique. If you're an architect, experience in sustainable design could help you stand out. If you're a financial planner with a special-needs child, you can offer your perspective and understanding to families in similar situations. If you transcribe recordings, find out what your client might be doing with your transcript and offer to tailor the results to make the results more useful. At the end of your interviews, you want to be able to describe your ideal clients in one sentence—"My best clients are civil litigation defense lawyers and related trial consultants."

Your Competitors or Your Colleagues?

Now that you've finished your reality check, you probably have
a clearer idea of what your clients really value and how you can
meet their needs. It's time to take a look around at others who
are doing something similar, remembering that—depending on
your business—your competitors, and your market, could be
anywhere in the world.

Competitors—the people who are also making a living doing
whatever it is that you enjoy so much—are more likely to be
your colleagues than your competition. (This is why it is so
important to learn from your reality-check interviews not only
what your clients need or want but also what would set you
apart—that unique added value that only you can offer.) I
started my business as a kind of librarian-for-hire, providing
research to analysts and business professionals. I soon realized
that, as with any high-value service, there were far more
potential clients than there were people who could serve them.

When I went to my first conference of the Association of
Independent Information Professionals (aiip.org), I expected to
be surrounded by cut-throat business owners trying to steal my
ideas or my clients. Imagine my relief when I realized that my
competition consisted of other research fanatics who love going
on an informational treasure hunt. We had a lot in common—
the challenges in communicating our value, managing difficult
clients, and handling cash flow and collections. In fact, I have
built decades-long friendships with "competitors" I have met
through AIIP. We give each other pep talks, we brainstorm
about difficult projects, and we subcontract or refer work to
each other whenever it seems appropriate.

While we work in the same general field, our clients range
from prison administrators to engineers, leaders of nonprofits,
lawyers, small-business owners, government officials, and
corporate strategic planners. Our specializations include such

disparate fields as patent research, focus groups, business valuation, grant writing, and medical-device safety. And our clients are all over the world—some of us focus on serving a local region and others market globally.

I have nothing to fear from my so-called competition; our areas of specialization rarely overlap. Instead, I see my fellow business owners as my colleagues. I can find someone to keep an eye on my business while I go on vacation. I can farm out a particular research project that requires skills I don't have. And I have plenty of people I can call on when I need to brainstorm about new marketing ideas or ways I can expand my services.

The Voice of Experience

Just as the reality-check interviews are instrumental in learning about your clients' needs and concerns, conversations with colleagues help you learn what challenges and issues you'll be dealing with yourself. "But why would someone help their competitor?" you ask. In fact, this is a useful litmus test to help you figure out if this is the line of work for you. Successful entrepreneurs know that they bring something unique to the marketplace, and they know that the more people who are in a field, the stronger that field becomes. (There's a joke about the first lawyer who came to town and had no business. Then a second lawyer came to town and both lawyers became wildly successful, because now people could sue each other.)

If you encounter colleagues who don't have an expansive view of their business and who don't want to share their experience with you, just move on. People with a constricted view and an attitude of fear don't offer you a useful perspective. The people you want to learn from are the ones who approach their work from an assumption of abundance— they understand that everyone has something unique to offer the marketplace. One aspect of social networks such as

Facebook and Twitter is that they help develop a culture that values and rewards sharing. Entrepreneurs who feel proprietary about their ideas often don't realize that they're losing business by "hoarding" information. By being generous with your time and ideas, you send the message to your clients that you know what your real value is and that it isn't lost by merely sharing ideas.

Finding Your People

How do you find your competitors/colleagues? The simple answer is to think like your clients. How would a client find someone like you? Would they search the web to find people in your line of business? Do they rely on referrals? If so, from whom? Where do they congregate?

If your business is one that must be done locally—chimney sweep or doula, for example—you can start by Googling your specialty and the name of your city—for example, "home inspector" Milwaukee. (Here's a power-searcher tip: Enclose phrases in quotation marks for more precise web search results.) Browse through the listings and see who has been in the business for a while. Whose web site looks professional? Have they specialized or expanded into related areas? Do they describe their background and what unique features they offer? Identify several colleagues whose businesses look vibrant and healthy.

But what if that technique doesn't work—your search turns up far too many listings or very few? This is when you start thinking like a client. If *you* were looking for someone with your expertise, where would you go? Who would you ask for a recommendation or referral?

- For a home inspector: local real estate agents
- For IT support services: local Chamber of Commerce, small-business events

- For a marketing consultant: the Business Marketing Association
- For a wedding planner: meetings of the Event Planners Association
- For a bookkeeper: CPAs, whose clients need ongoing support managing their books
- For a web designer: find other small businesses' web sites that you find appealing and see who is credited with designing the site (usually credited at the bottom of the home page)

"So, What's It Really Like?"

Once you've identified several other people who are doing something similar to your interest, call or e-mail them and tell them why you're reaching out to them—"the top real estate agent in the area recommended you" or "I saw that you gave a presentation recently on how small businesses can use social media to market themselves." Make it clear that you respect their time and that you value their expertise and perspective.

Prepare a list of questions that will help you figure out if this is the kind of business you would enjoy.

- Learn how they've expanded their businesses and how their businesses have changed over time. Do most people have to hire staff? If so, do you want your business to grow to the point where you'll be managing people?
- Is this the type of business that requires extensive travel? If so, does that sound like fun or does the thought of getting on an airplane every couple of weeks give you heartburn?
- How much investment was required to launch their business? How much overhead should you plan for? Will you need to rent an office or studio, or can you work from your home?

- Ask about how they find their customers. Do they get most of their clients from word-of-mouth referrals? If so, how do they create a buzz? Do they advertise heavily? Do they go to networking events to meet prospective clients? Remember that, whatever your business looks like, you'll always be marketing, although that doesn't necessarily mean TV ads, direct mail, or glad-handing it at a Chamber of Commerce meeting. For more on how to attract clients, see Chapter 10, *Brand "You."*

- How do they stay in contact with others who do what they do? Are there local get-togethers? A conference everyone attends? Getting to know others in your field is a great way to keep your skills fresh, build a network of peers you can collaborate with, and get a reality check when you run into a problem.

- Find out what they wish they had known when they started their business. What were their biggest surprises? What has been the most satisfying aspect of being an entrepreneur? Are there any pitfalls you should watch out for? Any common newbie mistakes?

After each conversation, write a thank you note by hand to each person. I know, I know—who does that sort of thing anymore? Answer: You do! It takes very little time to write a short note (enclose your business card if you have one), and people appreciate a tangible thank you. You can even create customized note cards for your business; companies like VistaPrint.com and Moo.com produce high-quality stationery in small quantities for around $25.

Keep in touch with everyone you've interviewed—your reality-check interviewees and your colleagues. They've already proven that they're engaged enough to share a bit of time with you; send them personalized notes every quarter, letting them know how your business is doing. They may turn into clients; at the least, they can offer feedback as you go forward and serve as a source of referrals. All that from just asking some questions!

Remember, too, that your business will evolve over time. I recommend reality-check interviews every five years; your clients' priorities and needs have probably changed over time, and you want to make sure you're continuing to offer something that they can't find anywhere else.

Five Questions for Discovering Your Client Base

- Are you attached to doing the same thing as an entrepreneur that you did as an employee?
- Have you talked with prospective clients to learn what they really value and what they'll pay?
- Do you understand what keeps your clients from achieving their goals?
- Are you open to providing new services as you learn more about your clients?
- Have you talked with peers to find out what their biggest challenges are?

5 Building the Framework

The White Rabbit put on his spectacles.
"Where shall I begin, please your Majesty?" he asked.
"Begin at the beginning," the King said, very gravely,
"and go on till you come to the end: then stop."

LEWIS CARROLL, FROM *ALICE'S ADVENTURES IN WONDERLAND*

Most entrepreneurs start out as one-person operations, and many find that this works just fine. Others begin their entrepreneurial life with a business partner on the assumption that two heads are better than one. Some people build their businesses by hiring employees or using freelancers extensively; others prefer to limit their growth to what they can do themselves. You'll have to make some decisions about how to structure your business before you open up shop, but you can also restructure later, as your needs and goals change.

Of course, this book can't take the place of advice from your lawyer and your accountant. Before you even consult with your advisors, consider these factors:

- Legal restrictions within your profession: Are you required to have a certain license or certification?

- Liabilities in the type of work you will do: Will you be doing work that is lawsuit-prone, like patent research?
- Type of business: Will you be providing a service that requires a permanent staff of employees?
- Tax advantages or disadvantages: What is the financial situation of your household? Your accountant can help you identify the most important tax issues to consider for you, your family, and your business.

Incorporating or Keeping It Simple

Entrepreneurs have four primary choices of business structure:

- Sole proprietorship
- Partnership
- Limited liability company
- Corporation

Each of these forms of business has its advantages and drawbacks, some of which will vary depending on where you live. Here's a quick description of each form at its simplest level.

- Sole proprietorship

  You and your business are essentially one; you're personally responsible for the profits and expenses of your business; you report your business income and expense through your personal income tax return. The majority of entrepreneurs start out as sole proprietors.

- Partnership

  Two or more people share the responsibilities, profits, and liabilities of the company; just as with sole proprietors, partners are not distinct from their business; you each report your business income and expense through your personal income tax return.

- Limited liability company
  A more structured version of a partnership (or sole proprietorship) that acts more like a corporation; the owner(s) is not personally responsible for corporate debts; business income and expenses are usually passed directly to your personal income tax return. An LLC can consist of just one person; it need not be a partnership. LLCs are regulated by each state; check with your state's Department of State for more information.

- Corporation
  A formal entity, legally independent of its owner(s) and able to enter into legally binding contracts; income is routinely distributed to you in the form of a salary; there are tax benefits after your income rises to a certain point; there is more recordkeeping and accounting required, and more filing requirements with various government agencies.

We'll go into more detail about the advantages and disadvantages of each form of business organization later in this chapter. But before we can get to the nitty-gritty aspects of limited liability companies vs. Subchapter S corporations, let's pause for a more strategic perspective on your business. The table below lists five issues and factors to consider about each when choosing an incorporated structure (limited liability company or corporation), a sole proprietorship, or partnership set-up. There are, of course, no correct answers; if you don't have a clear idea of any of the strategic concerns listed here, count that as another "vote" toward the sole proprietor route, for its simplicity and flexibility.

	Incorporate or Be a Sole Proprietor?	
Strategic Concern	Choose to incorporate/LLC if you:	Choose to be solo proprietor/ partnership if you:
Your vision of the size and nature of your business, now and in five years	Anticipate substantial year-to-year growth Expect to sell your interest in the business within a few years	Expect to earn a good salary but not to grow substantially beyond your (healthy / generous) salary goal
The level of control you want	Want to share responsibility, risk, rewards with partner(s) or employee(s)	Want to make all decisions Are comfortable identifying and taking strategic risks
How much formal structure you want or need	Want to have an entity that is entirely separate from your household Don't mind additional accounting and recordkeeping expense	Want to have a simple structure that allows for easy monitoring of financial situation Don't mind doing your own routine accounting and recordkeeping
Your potential liability	Are involved in a product or service with high liability	Are comfortable with the usual risks of any business enterprise
Your exit strategy	Expect to build a brand-based (vs. personal-based) business that can be sold successfully to another owner for additional income	See your business more as a consultancy than a "company" and do not expect to derive income from the business when you close it

Should You Partner with Your Partner or with Your Pal?

As those of us in marriages or other life partnerships know, our spouses are involved in our business at some level, whether or not we or they want it. They experience the impact of cash flow fluctuations along with us; they help troubleshoot our tech problems; they're invariably gracious when we answer a client call during dinner; and we even expect them to listen patiently to our stories of the thrill of victory and the agony of defeat.

Partnering with Your Partner

In some situations, life partners become business partners as well. They find it rewarding to create a business with the person they know the best and whom they trust and love. They want to share the joys and the fears of entrepreneurship, and they value the synergy they bring to life's challenges.

If you think this sounds like a good arrangement, think about how you and your partner interact now, and consider how your relationship styles will mesh in a business. As difficult as these questions are, addressing them now helps ensure that your business issues don't become marital issues.

- How well do you communicate with each other? Overall, do you each feel "heard" by the other?
- How well do you handle conflict? How do you each deal with anger and fear?
- How do you make decisions—both large and small? Does one person usually defer to the other?
- How do you handle disagreements about choices? How strong are your negotiation skills?

In addition, consider how much time and energy each of you expects to invest in your business. Are you both planning on working full time on the business? Will you have income from another source while your business grows and begins to generate profit? And finally, do you enjoy spending all day with your significant other, or do you need to have time alone or with others? How will you support your individual working styles while working together?

Partnering with Your Pal

Perhaps you hatched a great business plan with two close friends. All of you are excited about it, and you can't wait to get started. The other two friends are dating each other and you've all known each other since college, so you figure there's no reason why this can't work. Or perhaps you're both refugees from the "traditional" world of employment, looking for new options; you've known each other for years and figure that two heads are better than one.

Personal chemistry is one aspect of successful partnerships among friends that is difficult to assess ahead of time. How do your personalities mesh when things get stressful? Does one person want to make quick decisions and another need time to ponder the possibilities? Carol Lee-Roark, of Hyalite Environmental, LLP, has found a way to successfully maintain a business partnership with two close friends. In fact, as she says, "We couldn't be happier." I asked her to what she attributed her success.

This may work because none of us is overtaxed with ambition—we each have as our goal "to make enough money to pay my bills and support my hobbies," with the emphasis being on quality of life. One of our starting concepts was that we never wanted to hear the phrase "grow the company" again, having been "growed" to death, and merged and acquired and sold too often in our previous careers. And we agreed that we never want to have payroll and employees. We have three home offices, electronically connected, and we try to do the best work in our field with the best quality of life as well. Personality-wise, we are totally compatible—mellow and easygoing about relationships, but Type-A about doing things right.

What I think was key is that we already knew each other in a working relationship; the other two were on a team I managed. We knew each other's work-related strengths and weaknesses, and we had enough years together to have built a shared collection of experiences and insights. As a result of working together, we became friends, and eventually we became business partners. We know who shouldn't be called before 10:00 in the morning, who needs to be reined in from doing too much research, and who is chronically overscheduled.

Our partnership agreement pretty much sets us up as cooperating individual consultants—we can contribute time, effort, and so on as we wish, and anyone can take their ball and go home whenever they wish. On the other hand, we

*are not proprietary about clients and projects, which I've
seen in other partnerships and which seems really difficult
and hostile to me. We figure that we each should be able to
take over and do any job, and to make the difference among
the three of us invisible and seamless to our clients. We
share all projects—none of us thinks that any project or
client would be better off without input from the other
partners. We do have arguments about technical issues, but
these are debates in which we are discussing a specific issue,
and more often than not we each end up switching opinions
a few times and eventually beating out the most
appropriate solution.*

Partnering Precautions

It may be tempting to bring in our partner or a friend as a
kind of buffer or backup. Maybe we want someone else to take
some of the responsibility and assume some of the risk.

- "He offers me lots of advice about my business, so why not
  formalize it?"
- "We've known each other through a professional
  association and we have a similar idea for a business. Why
  not have a business together?"
- "I'll do all the work and she'll do all the marketing and
  administrative work, which I hate."

Do any of these sound familiar? If so, think twice about your
motivations for bringing in a partner. Unless there is a real
synergy between you and your potential business partner, two
people means half the profit without the assurance of twice the
income.

If what you really want is support, either create an advisory
or mastermind group to serve as a sounding board or negotiate
with your spouse for lots of support regarding your business.
Identify what aspects of your business you can successfully

outsource (see Chapter 6, *Managing Yourself and Your Business*) and what aspects you can approach with a more creative perspective (see Chapter 11, *The Reluctantly Strategic Entrepreneur*).

> *If you plan on eventually selling your business, you will need to incorporate at some point.*

Marge King, of InfoRich Group, Inc., has some useful advice for spouses or close friends who are considering forming a business partnership, based on personal experience and a course she teaches on small business start-ups.

In one of my business classes, I brought in an attorney, a banker, an accountant, and an insurance agent to talk about real-world issues. When asked about going into business with a family member or a close friend, the surprisingly strong and universal reaction from the panel was, "Do NOT do it!" No one on the panel could think of a successful company formed of family members or close friends, with the exception of some husband-wife teams. I am sad to say that my experience is in line with this.

That said, here are some of the issues I encourage my students to consider regarding a partnership with a spouse or close friend.

First, have a well-defined exit strategy developed before you start the business. Make sure that you agree on the answers to questions such as these:

- *If one person calls it quits, will the business survive?*
- *Will it be bought by the other owners? If so, how will you value it?*
- *Can a partner sell his/her stake to an outsider?*

- *Will the person leaving the business accept payments over time for his/her share of the partnership?*
- *What will happen if someone dies? Will the person's heirs suddenly become your business "partner"? Will they be involved in the day-to-day activities?*
- *Do not operate it as an "equal" partnership or stock ownership; someone needs to be the boss and make the final decision.*

Everyone needs to write down their expectations of how they anticipate benefiting from the business and how they expect to see it run. Who will decide issues such as salaries, expenses, operations, company policies, and so on?

Looking at all these areas before forming a partnership will help everyone gain insight into where problems may arise and will allow the group to address these in advance. Once you have agreement on these issues, develop a business plan that includes this information and make sure everyone agrees to it. Then you can refer back to it when there are disputes or issues. And, yes, there will be disputes and issues.

Protecting Your Social Security Number
As a sole proprietor, you'll be asked for your Social Security number by the accounting offices of vendors and clients. They need your "Taxpayer Identification Number," which in your case is usually your SSN, in order to file an IRS Form 1099 on which they report how much they paid you during the year. (1099s must be filed by anyone who pays an individual at least $600 annually, supposedly to ensure that you do not cheat by under-reporting your income as a sole proprietor.) Because your SSN can be used to commit all kinds of fraud,

> *some entrepreneurs are reluctant to give out that number. You can get around this remote but real possibility by requesting an Employer Identification Number (EIN) from the IRS. You don't have to be an employer; you don't even have to be incorporated. You just have to fill out IRS Form SS-4, Application for Employer Identification Number, which you can download from www.irs.gov, and your EIN will be mailed to you. Then you can provide your EIN to clients instead of your Social Security number. Your clients will still have to fill out a Form 1099 on the payments they made to you, but at least your SSN will remain secure.*

What Kind of Animal Are You?

As you read through the following section on different business structures and formats, consider which would make sense for you, whether you expect to be in a partnership or operating solo. If you want to work with others, you can create a partnership, an LLC, or a corporation. In fact, you could even structure a group in which some members are employees and others are owners. Likewise, if you want to work alone, you could form a sole proprietorship, a corporation (with you as the sole employee), or a single-person LLC. What matters is not the number of people involved as much as what you want to accomplish with your business structure.

As I have said elsewhere, talk with your lawyer and accountant before you form your business. Your personal situation may dictate one business structure over another.

Sole Proprietorship

This is the simplest way to start your business and the one that most entrepreneurs opt for (or default to), at least at the beginning. In essence, you and your business are the same entity—you can operate under a trade name, but your clients and vendors are dealing with you as an individual. The legal agreements you enter into, and the contracts you sign, obligate you personally.

> *The process of putting your ideas into writing helps you make your vision a reality; it's a tangible commitment to yourself.*

The biggest advantage of a sole proprietorship is simplicity. You report your income to the IRS on the familiar personal income tax Form 1040, using Schedule C to itemize your business expenses. Bookkeeping is relatively simple, and the only mid-year filings required are the quarterly payments of your estimated income tax.

One of the main reasons some entrepreneurs eventually change their business structure is that sole proprietors are legally liable for all the debts of the company. Companies to which you owe money can go after your personal assets (yes, that's your house we're talking about) if you do not pay your bills. In addition, some business expenses cannot be fully deducted from your income, such as health insurance payments. You may also find it more difficult to obtain a business loan or line of credit from a bank as a sole proprietor than you would as an independent company. You can't sell a sole proprietorship business because you and the business are one, so if you plan on eventually selling your business, you will need to incorporate at some point. And finally, once your business is successful and you're earning a substantial income, you run a higher risk of being audited by the IRS as a sole proprietor than you would as a corporation or LLC.

Partnership

You can form a partnership with someone who will take an active role in the business or with someone who provides some or all of the funding but doesn't participate in day-to-day operations. Partnerships are easy to set up, although you should plan to spend a good deal of time working through the partnership agreement. As with a sole proprietorship, the income of the business is reported on each partner's individual tax return, simplifying the accounting and bookkeeping burden. Some of the downsides of partnerships are that you and your partner are personally liable for the debts of the company, and you are each liable for the actions of the other. If one of you wants to leave the partnership, the business itself has to be re-formed. And unless you agree ahead of time that one of you has 51 percent ownership, you may run into problems when you and your partner disagree about an important decision.

Limited Liability Company

LLCs are relatively new entities, designed to provide both the tax benefits of incorporation and the flexibility of a sole proprietorship or partnership. Limited liability companies offer limited protection from personal liability, which makes them an attractive alternative to a partnership. However, like corporations, LLCs have some additional filing requirements and less operational flexibility than sole proprietorships or partnerships. The IRS doesn't recognize LLCs, although all state governments do. This means that you'll probably be treated as a sole proprietor by the IRS when it comes to taxing your income. Individual states vary in how they handle LLC income, so check the web site of your state's Department of State or Department of Corporations (in some states, the Department of Revenue handles business regulations).

Corporation

Several types of corporations can be formed, but the one most relevant to entrepreneurs is the "Subchapter S" corporation, a specific type of corporation best suited for most small companies. Corporations have the advantage of existing separately from their owners or partners. This means that the assets of the owner—that's you—are at least somewhat protected from the debts of the corporation. That does not mean you can spend like there's no tomorrow and escape the consequences when the bills come due, but it does help shield you if, heaven forbid, your company goes into bankruptcy.

Unlike a sole proprietorship or partnership, a corporation can be transferred to a partner or sold outright, which can be an important consideration if you think you might someday sell your business. There are also some tax benefits to incorporating, and if your revenue is high enough, you somewhat reduce the risk of an audit if you're operating as a corporation rather than as a sole proprietorship. If you plan on hiring employees, you may want to be incorporated for liability and tax reasons.

My Newly Incorporated Life

On the advice of my accountant and my lawyer, I was a sole proprietor for the first ten years of my business. It kept my life simple. I could manage both my personal and business finances through accounting software. Preparing my own tax returns was relatively simple, but then, I do have a mathematical bent.

After ten years I decided to revisit the form my business should take. I consulted with a CPA and, on his advice, finally incorporated. The process itself was pretty straightforward, and doing it at the end of the year made the transition fairly simple. I continue to handle the day-to-day accounting activities myself—things like paying bills, generating invoices, and tracking overdue payments. Then I e-mail a copy of my accounts to a bookkeeper at the end of the month, and she handles all the reports, filings, and deductions. At the end of the year, I send my balance sheet and P&L (profit and loss) statements to my accountant, who prepares my personal and corporate income tax filings.

There are several advantages of incorporating at this point in my career:

- I can put more money into a tax-free retirement fund.
- I've reduced my personal liability.
- I've reduced my chances of being audited by the IRS (knock wood).
- I can write off some expenses that I couldn't write off as a sole proprietor.

These are the downsides of incorporating:

- I can't do my tax filings myself (I know—most people wouldn't see this as a disadvantage, but I can't help it—I'm a math nerd).
- I have to be extra careful about not mingling my business and personal accounts.
- I have to pay a bookkeeper to handle my monthly filings, whereas as a sole proprietor I could do virtually all of the accounting myself.

The bottom line is that I'm glad I incorporated when I did. It saves me money and gives me a sense of security that I'm keeping my business and my personal accounts entirely separate. I recommend that you have a heart-to-heart talk with your accountant before you start your business and then every few years thereafter. Your financial situation will change, your life situation may change, and the tax laws will undoubtedly change, so it makes sense to get a reality check periodically.

Business Plans and Other Pipe Dreams

Everyone starting a business is told that it's critical to write a detailed business plan. If you don't have a business plan, how will you know which way you are going and when you have gotten there? How can you ask a potential lender for heaps of cash or launch an online fundraising campaign if you haven't spelled out what you want to do with the money when you get it? You'll certainly need a business plan—complete with financial projections—to apply for money from a bank or credit union, or even from family or friends. If you do decide to borrow money, include in your business plan how you plan to pay back the loan and what you'll use the money for.

Whether or not you're planning to borrow money, writing a business plan can be a useful reality check. You'll use your business plan to set goals for how much income you intend to bring in, how much you need to pay yourself as a salary, how much overhead you'll have, where and how you'll find clients, and so on. Your business plan should be optimistic and realistic—there's no sense aiming low just so you can meet your goal, nor is it wise to plan on earning $500,000 the first year.

> *The more time you spend on marketing at the beginning of your business, the sooner clients will start calling you.*

Another reason for writing a business plan is that the process of putting your ideas into writing helps you make that vision a reality. It's a tangible commitment—to yourself if no one else—that you take this new business seriously, that you intend to make this enterprise thrive. It also enables you to think through what you need to do and how you intend to accomplish your goals. One of the characteristics of most successful entrepreneurs is the ability to see not only the big picture but also the details, and to pay attention to all the little things that have to happen in order for the business to succeed. Of course, at some point down the road as your business grows and matures, you'll probably notice that real life has overtaken your well-designed plan and your business has moved into areas you hadn't foreseen. That's OK—it's an indication that you're able to recognize changes in the marketplace and your client base, and adapt to new situations. That original business plan helped you organize your thoughts, plan your actions, anticipate challenges and opportunities, and get started; you can update it as your business evolves.

There's no single way to go about writing a business plan. In fact, unless you intend to use it to apply for a loan, the only people who see it may be you and your business advisor, typically an accountant and/or a lawyer, or your business coach. Don't sweat the format; focus on thinking through what's involved in getting your business going.

Plenty of web sites give pointers about writing business plans. A good place to start is the U.S. Small Business Administration's web site (sba.gov). There's a section called "Starting & Managing a Business," which includes a number of guides and articles on business plans. (Just type the words **starting managing business** in the SBA site search box to find this section.) You can also find large collections of resources at SCORE (formerly Service Corps of Retired Executives, score.org) and the Ewing Marion Kauffman Foundation (entrepreneurship.org).

Business Plan Checklist

Your business plan may be polished and formal, or it could be a simple write-up of how you envision your company in its first year. In either case, you should answer—or at least think carefully about—each of the following questions.

- Why are you starting this business?
  Are you excited about the idea of making a living doing what you love to do? Or are you starting a business because you feel like you have no other choice? Do you feel forced into this or are you stepping forward to a new challenge?
- What service or product are you providing to clients?
  You'll probably not be doing the same kind of work as when you were employed, which means that the skills and expertise that are valued in the workplace are not necessarily those that clients value. What are you offering to your clients that they can't find or do themselves?
- Who are your potential clients?
  Do you expect to find most of your clients locally? Do you need to have face-to-face interactions, or can you use voice and video calls with clients across the country or around the world?
- How will you attract clients?
  Most entrepreneurs find that cold calls, direct mail, and unsolicited e-mails are not effective ways of building a business. How will you start the word-of-mouth marketing that will sustain your business? Are you willing to invest a quarter or third of your time in marketing?
- How have you confirmed that your clients actually want, need, and value this service?
  Have you conducted reality-check interviews with people you think are typical of your potential clients? What did you learn? Will you have to educate prospects about why they need you, or will your value be clear to them?
- How many repeat clients do you expect by the end of your first year?
  It takes far less time and energy to retain a client than to gain a new one. Will your clients want to use your services

or products regularly? How will you encourage repeat business?

- Who are your competitors?
  Every business has competitors, even if the competition is, "I'll do it myself." How are your clients meeting their needs now? How are you distinct from others in your field?

- How will you price your services or products?
  Do you have an idea of what others charge for similar services or products? How can you offer something of more value? Are you comfortable with charging people what you consider a fair price for your time and expertise?

- What will your overhead be for the first year?
  While you can't anticipate all your expenses, be sure that your fees are high enough to cover the essentials for a successful business. These include not only your phone and Internet costs, health insurance, web site expenses, and so on, but also membership in a professional association, attendance at conferences your clients attend, and the cost for professional development workshops.

- What is your expected revenue the first year? And after that?
  How big do you see your business becoming? Do you expect it to support you after the first year? Do you want your business to grow larger over the years?

- If you're doing this full time, how will you cover all your living expenses for your first six months?
  Do you have savings you can tap into until your business begins to show a profit? What expenses can you reduce or eliminate while you're in the start-up phase?

- What are your personal strengths and weaknesses as a business owner?
  What aspects of running a business sound the most intimidating to you? What can you do to build your

familiarity and comfort level with the skills you need? What parts of being an entrepreneur excite you the most? What can you do to expand those facets of your business?

- What are your strengths and weaknesses in this market? When you look at others in your field, where do you stand out? Do you have more years of experience than others? A wider variety of skills? A familiarity with a number of industries? Do you need to refresh your skills or build new ones in order to be competitive?

Remember, there are no right or wrong answers. Use these questions as a framework for creating a business plan that is meaningful to you and that can serve as a roadmap for your first year.

What about My Steady Paycheck?

One of the first considerations when planning to open up shop is whether to quit your regular job (if you have one) before you launch. There are two schools of thought about this: Some entrepreneurs say that the only way you can survive financially the first year is to run your new business on the side; others say that the only way to get traction is to focus on your business full time. Below are some of the advantages and disadvantages of each choice.

Full-Time Entrepreneur

This is certainly the scariest option. You go from a steady income and employee benefits like health insurance and paid vacations to zero—or rather, to put it in a more positive light, to a full focus on your new business. This option works best if:

- Someone else in your household is bringing in a steady income.
- You've set aside enough money to live on for six to nine months.

- You already have at least one regular client, such as your last employer.

On the positive side, working on your business full time means that word-of-mouth referrals get started that much faster. You can devote more time to marketing, which takes time to show results. The more time you can spend on marketing at the beginning of your business, the sooner those clients will start calling you.

One advantage of taking the plunge and working full time for yourself is less tangible but just as important: By devoting yourself full time to your business, you demonstrate to yourself and to the people you interact with that you are committed to creating a joyful, successful business and to providing high-quality products or professional services to your clients. Certainly part-timers can be just as committed, but it's substantially harder to maintain that level of enthusiasm, creativity, and persistence if you're juggling your new business, an existing job, and at least a minimal personal life.

As for the downsides of going full time, the most obvious one is financial. Unless you already have clients lined up, don't expect to be able to pay yourself a salary for at least a few months. The first year is likely to be lean. Before I quit my job and started my (full-time) research business, I spent a year focused on lowering my living expenses. I got into the habit of not eating out as frequently, not practicing "shopping therapy," and generally learning that a lot of my discretionary spending was unnecessary. This made my first year in business easier to handle because I could get by with substantially less income than I had been earning in my last job. I also figured out ahead of time how much money I needed each month just to pay the bills, and I banked six months' worth of living expenses, which I drew from when I didn't have many clients yet still had to pay my overhead expenses.

Part-Time Entrepreneur

There are two kinds of part-time business owners: people who have another part-time job and people who choose to work only part time. The latter often have childcare or eldercare obligations or health limitations that prevent them from working full time. With discipline and flexibility, you can create a business that works around and blends with the rest of your life.

If you're juggling caring for others with running your business, consider hiring someone to help with your home responsibilities during the day—even (especially!) if you work at home. You'll still be available for emergencies, but you're freed up to fully focus on creating a way to express your talents and get paid for it.

Taking a client's call while the kids are trying to put doll clothes on the cat is doomed to failure. One of the essential tasks of someone with others in the house during the day is to teach them that when your office door is closed, you can be interrupted only if someone has severed a limb, the house is on fire, or you are ready for a break.

The steady income and benefits of a part-time employee job are a nice safety net while you're building your business. However, it's easy to start seeing your part-time job as your *real* job. Will you think of your employment as supplementing your new business or vice versa? Which do you want? Do you want to eventually be able to quit your job and have your business support you, or is your goal to happily work part time for an employer and part time for yourself?

Moonlighting Employee

Working full time at a job and running your business on weekends and evenings is difficult, at least if you plan to eventually grow beyond a weekend-and-evening enterprise. Almost by definition, most of your energy and time will be focused on your regular job, even if it's a job you don't enjoy. In fact, it probably takes even more of your energy if it's a job you are not happy in! That said, if what you want is a very part-time business, this may be a great choice, giving you a steady salary from your day job and occasional additional revenue from your side business.

Taking the Leap

It's easy to feel daunted by all the preliminary tasks—writing a business plan, setting up your office, talking with a lawyer or accountant, identifying your client base, determining your niche, and so on. I like to compare all this preliminary work to taking up a new sport. For the first few weeks, you're going to be stiff and sore; it seems like all pain and no gain. But once you get your muscles toned up, you start seeing dramatic results. Likewise, all these administrative and strategic planning tasks are hard at first—they are new jobs, they are unfamiliar, and they require you to sit down and really think about what you want. But once you've gone through the process, it's a lot easier to continue. You'll always have administrative and high-level management responsibilities; now is the time to learn how to handle them and to start feeling comfortable in your new roles.

Susan Doran, a wise friend, once told me that starting a business feels like standing on the edge of a cliff, looking down at the ground far below. Then you suddenly realize that what appeared to be empty space is actually a path up, or that it's merely a single step down to the earth, or that you can fly. I couldn't agree more.

Five Key Questions When Forming Your Business

- Does your business involve significant liability? Do you run any meaningful risk of being sued?
- Do you intend to eventually sell your business to someone else?
- If you're considering a partnership, what does each person bring to the business?
- Can you afford a full-time focus on your business, or will this be a part-time business?
- What are your goals for the year? What do you want your business to look like?

6 Managing Yourself and Your Business

> "Now, here, you see, it takes all the running you can do,
> to keep in the same place.
> If you want to get somewhere else,
> you must run at least twice as fast as that!"
>
> LEWIS CARROLL, FROM *THROUGH THE LOOKING-GLASS*

One of the aspects of being self-employed that I appreciate daily is not reporting to a boss. It's true that my clients are, collectively, my employer, and I strive to build my business around what my clients want and value. What I don't have is someone to whom I have to report, someone who holds me accountable for showing up to work on time, putting in a full day's work, and adjusting my schedule to her priorities. I don't have an annual performance review, nor do I have to write them for people who report to me. In fact, I don't have anyone reporting to me. Woo-hoo!

The flip side is that I'm responsible for managing myself, my time, my priorities, and my business. This means that if I miss a deadline or don't follow through on something, I'm accountable for and live with the consequences. Likewise, I need to make sure I'm staying current in my field—reading what thought leaders say, attending events to hone my professional skills, and constantly asking myself if I'm on top of issues that affect me and that affect my clients. Self-management also means that I get to define what "success" looks like. As a one-person business, I can focus on what's particularly gratifying and enriching for me; that usually includes having a healthy income, a flexible schedule, work in which I feel that I can make a difference, and the privilege of working from the beauty and serenity of my home. This chapter goes into more detail about each of these aspects of managing yourself and your business so that you enjoy all the rewards of working for yourself.

Time Management

Unstructured time is difficult for some entrepreneurs. You show up at your office in the morning and find none of the usual cues to buckle down and start working—no ringing phones, no voices from the next cubicle, no boss walking by asking about the TPS report that's due at noon. Unless you have a client's project staring you in the face, or some administrative tasks that absolutely have to be done, you'll need to create your own structure for each day.

> *Self-management means that I get to define what "success" looks like.*

If you find that the days keep slipping away from you and you feel like you haven't accomplished anything by 5:30 P.M., work on being mindful of how you spend your day. You may want to keep a diary for a week and see how you spend every hour. (There are many free time-tracking apps for mobile phones that help you monitor your time.) At the end of the week, add up the time and see where it went. Some people find that working at home creates all kinds of little time sinks. "I'll just run out now and do the grocery shopping while the store isn't crowded." "I'll just take care of the dry cleaning and run a few loads of wash." "I'll just meet a friend for a quick cup of coffee." It's great to be able to get the laundry done while you work, but if that turns into two hours of tidying up the house, then you're not working. Likewise, the flexibility to meet friends, go for a walk, and take care of personal errands during the week is a benefit of being an entrepreneur, but if you find that you're spending a quarter of your week this way, it's time to rethink your schedule.

Know when you are most productive and schedule the critical tasks then. Do you need long periods of uninterrupted time in order to concentrate? Set aside a day during which you turn off your phone, close down your e-mail app, and do nothing but what needs to get accomplished. Do you usually have an energy slump mid-afternoon? Schedule a walk around the block at 3:00 every afternoon.

> *Know when you are most productive and schedule your critical tasks then.*

Home-based entrepreneurs who have children at home find that the issue of boundaries is particularly important. There are times when you have to put your head down and focus all your attention on getting a report written or an estimate out the door. And there are times when your child comes home from school and needs to tell you something (or just wants to reconnect). You'll need to create some way to indicate to your family when you can't be interrupted, regardless of whether or not you look like you're working.

"Vacation? What Vacation?"

Many entrepreneurs find the idea of vacation daunting. Not only is our time off unpaid but we often don't have administrative support to handle our clients while we're away. What will happen if a client calls? How will I keep up with e-mail and still enjoy my time off?

Over the last two decades, I've taken a wide range of approaches to getting away from my business and relaxing. I appreciate the flexibility that I get from being my own boss; I can structure my vacation time so that my business continues while I'm away from the office. In some years, I can simply tell my regular clients that I'm going offline for two weeks to build hiking trails in the mountains, and I know that I can resume my projects when I return. Then there are times when it would cause me more stress than it was worth to be out of touch with clients during vacations. I remind myself that I *choose* to have clients who need more hand-holding, and I schedule an hour or two a day for work. I focus on business issues for a set amount of time each day, and can then put work aside for the rest of the day.

Whenever you leave your office for more than a day or two, consider the impacts your absence will have on your business.

- You are the most important asset of your business
  It's important that you take time off regularly. Give yourself a break from thinking about accounts payable, when that client is going to call back, and how you're going to generate new business. It can be refreshing to realize that everything can wait for a day or two.
- Meet the expectations of your clients.
  My hairdresser encourages her customers to book appointments through her online scheduling service, which allows her to take time off without needing to respond to phone calls.

- Use an upcoming vacation or business trip as a reason to reach out to clients.
  Tell them when you will be out of the office and ask if they need your services before you go. I have often found that this generates additional work; even when it does not, I have had one more opportunity to reach out and remind my clients that I am still around and in business.
- Take advantage of predictable lulls in your business.
  Is there a particular time of year when you know your clients aren't as likely to need you? Are the summer months usually quiet? Is the end of the year slow for you? As you become familiar with the ebb and flow of your market, take advantage of the down times to give yourself a break, too.

Turning Yourself Off at Night

It seems that there are two kinds of entrepreneurs: some have difficulty sitting at their desk from 9:00 A.M. to 5:00 P.M., working all alone; others have trouble leaving the office at the end of the day and tend to let their work take over all their available time. Figure out which type you are and develop a strategy for sticking to the office hours that you set for yourself.

At the end of your work day, turn off your phone ringer and e-mail alerts so that you're not tempted to respond to after-hours calls. If your clients discover that you'll pick up the phone at any hour, they'll call at any hour, and that way madness lies. Instead, really *leave* the office at the end of the day.

As a way to remind themselves that the office is closed, several home-based entrepreneurs I know toss a towel over their computer at the end of the day or the week. You might want to try some of these techniques:

- Make a commitment with your spouse or partner that you'll commit to regular office hours with consistent starting and closing times.

- Consciously close down your business at the end of the day. Spend five or ten minutes straightening up your desk, wrapping up any loose ends, reviewing your schedule for the next day, and lining up your to-do list of specific actions you need to take for each of your current projects. By organizing your office at the end of the day, you ensure that you can start working as soon as you return in the morning.
- Schedule an activity that requires you to leave work at a reasonable hour. If you've wanted to get in shape, find a yoga class that meets at 6:00 P.M. or meet a friend at the gym.
- Set up a reminder that it's time to end the day. That might be telling the kids that they can come into your office any time after 5:00 or, as I do, setting your phone to start chirping like a cricket when it's time to end the work day. If you need a more heavy-handed approach, consider using an app like Freedom or LeechBlock, which can be programmed to disable your computer's Internet connection at a certain time every day.

Staying Sharp

Employees often have access to programs within their organization through which they can acquire new expertise, stay updated on what others in their field are doing, and keep their professional skills fresh. One-person businesses don't have the luxury of a training department, but we can find ways to continually enhance our skills, too.

It's likely that there are people in your town who are passionate about the same thing you are. One way to find them is to watch for listings of get-togethers through networking services like MeetUp.com. Identify the professional or trade association to which other people in your field belong, and join their local chapter. Need help identifying a relevant association?

Your local public library probably has the *Encyclopedia of Associations*, an exhaustive directory of groups ranging from interior designers to interpreters for the deaf and eldercare lawyers. The American Society of Association Executives (asaecenter.org) also provides a searchable directory of associations in its Gateway to Associations service.

> *Marketing does not lend itself to being outsourced; we entrepreneurs are selling ourselves, and we best understand what value we're offering to our clients.*

You may want to include money in your budget to attend your association's annual conference. While the cost, including travel, may run $1500 or $2000, this investment is what sets you apart from others in your field and ensures that you can offer your clients more value and new services. Many of these associations focus on updating their participants' skills and helping them succeed professionally. This kind of support and learning only happens at gatherings of people who are passionate about what they do. I consider my annual attendance at a professional conference to be part of the cost of doing business, and I set my prices so that I have the income that allows me to attend.

Outsourcing What You Can

As a one-person business, the most valuable resource you manage is your time, and your responsibility as the head of your company is to make sure you're using that resource wisely. What aspects of your business could someone else do better and more efficiently than you, and, if you were relieved of that responsibility, what else could you do with that time and focus that would be more valuable?

For some entrepreneurs, one the most onerous tasks is marketing. In my opinion, marketing is one area that does *not* lend itself to being outsourced; we entrepreneurs are selling ourselves, and we best understand what value we're offering to our clients. Chapter 9, *Your (Fabulous) Marketing Plan,* goes into more detail about marketing approaches that feel comfortable for you.

Other aspects of running a business—accounting, designing your business card, routine scheduling—are easier to hand over to someone else because they don't require the same ongoing, in-depth knowledge of your clients and others in your market. Consider how much time you can (and want to) spend developing your skills. Developing a logo is something a graphic designer can do fairly quickly; how much time would you need to create a professional-looking design yourself? If you're not interested in the details of accounting, you can hire someone whose business it is to keep on top of the ins and outs of the tax laws.

Consider bartering with other entrepreneurs; you may know someone who doesn't mind following up on your outstanding invoices in exchange for you editing her client newsletter. Be sure that you have clear agreements when you exchange services. Agree before beginning work how much time you each expect to spend on the work, what the expected outcomes are, and what the limits are on what you can do. In addition to getting your onerous tasks taken care of by others, you expand your network and have an opportunity to see how other small businesses operate.

Making More Mistakes

Let's start with a given: No one is perfect. We've all made assumptions that turned out to be wrong. We've all said really dumb things sometimes. We've all tried something that we've failed at—sometimes spectacularly. The secret of success is to recognize that every mistake you make means that you have one more piece of information about the world. "Ah, I have learned that describing myself as 'a Roto-Rooter for your soul' doesn't resonate with most people." "Contrary to my expectation, engineering firms aren't interested in bookkeeping services." If you aren't making any mistakes, you aren't taking any risks and you'll never make the breakthroughs that come with taking (reasonable) chances.

The secret to success through failure is to know when to throw all your energy into something and when to step back and evaluate your effort. Yoda had it right when it comes to testing an idea: "Do or do not. There is no try." This is particularly applicable as you're figuring out how to build your business and attract clients. Rather than deciding that you will "try marketing to architects," draw up a marketing plan that spells out what "marketing to architects" looks like. This could include your measurable goals (three new active clients within six months), the specific actions you'll take (interview four architects to learn how they currently handle their social media marketing, join and volunteer with a local group of architects), and "pause points" every few weeks, when you stop and evaluate what you've learned so far, and consider whether and how you need to pivot in your approach. During your test period, pay attention to what results you're getting, and make adjustments as necessary to move toward your goal. By being purposeful in your approach, devoting all the time and energy required, and giving yourself enough time for your approach to succeed, you'll gain valuable insights at the end of any marketing effort, even if the results you get are not the results you expected.

Although I don't always like it, being an entrepreneur has given me a much deeper understanding of my strengths and weaknesses. I have a much better appreciation now of my range of skills than I did when I was an employee. I also have a frighteningly clear vision of my tendency to procrastinate, something that was mitigated when I had a more structured work environment. And I've learned that, although I'll always be an introvert, being shy is a habit that can be shifted with practice.

Here are some of the areas that often bring out the best or the worst in entrepreneurs. Keep in mind that these are not immutable personal characteristics; they're just behaviors that can be changed:

- Keeping your perspective.
  Can you maintain a focus on both the big picture of your business and the day-to-day operational issues?
- Handling feedback.
  Can you accept compliments from others gracefully? Can you listen to negative comments with the attitude that there may be something to learn, while discerning what input isn't useful?
- Getting things done.
  Can you manage your time effectively, distinguishing between the urgent and the important? Can you turn your ideas into action?

Getting the Important Things Done
Marcy Phelps, owner of Phelps Research, is a colleague and good friend who introduced me to the principle of Getting Things Done, or GTD. Here, in her words, is how she gets the important things in her life done.

> "I'm a big fan of David Allen's methodology for "stress-free productivity," as he describes in his book, *Getting Things Done*, and on his web site, GettingThingsDone.com. GTD kept me sane during

the period of my life when I was running a business, writing a book, and serving as president of an international professional association. Using GTD to organize and track the tasks, e-mails, events, notes, and files for all these really big projects helped me survive—and sleep at night.

I was initially drawn to GTD because it's basically all about gathering, organizing, and managing information—which is what I do for a living. I stay with it because of the insights I get about my life and my work. For example, during the process of taking stock of, documenting, and organizing all those bits of information, something happens. I start making sense of things, seeing connections, and visualizing "what if?" and "why not?"

Then there's the Project List. Keeping an inventory of all current projects not only helps make sure I'm actually getting things done; it offers insights into roadblocks and changes in priorities. What's being neglected—and why? Finally, the Weekly Review is the time to set the course for the upcoming week to make sure I control my time and it doesn't control me. It's also when I think about possibilities and move those Someday/Maybe items into action. It's amazing what your mind—and you—will accomplish once you clear the clutter!"

Living Large

There are different ways of living life richly. You can spend money as fast as you make it and wind up living from paycheck to paycheck (or, as an entrepreneur, from client payment to client payment). Or you can focus on finding richness and wealth in whatever situation you're in, in ways that don't involve cash. The first six months or year of a new business are going to be hard; you'll be working like crazy to find new clients, and you'll probably be spending more money than you take in. You can react to this by feeling desperate, making cold calls to random prospects, accepting work for which you aren't qualified or that is far below your regular rate, and generally losing your cool. Or you can focus on the ways in which you *are* wealthy, right now at the beginning of your life as an entrepreneur. Here are a few of the riches I reminded myself I had during my first, lean year:

- I can set my own schedule and take time to walk the dogs during the day.
- I get to meet all kinds of interesting people—prospective clients, colleagues, and other people with whom I work.
- I can play music as loud as I want, all day long.
- I can try out new ideas without running them by my boss for approval.
- I don't have to sit through committee meetings.
- I don't have to manage, motivate, or inspire anyone other than myself.
- I can nurture friendships and connect with people in new ways.

I continue to enjoy these riches as my business has grown because I have built my business with the intention of living a life in keeping with my values. You can pull together your own list of things that you find gratifying and that make your life fulfilling. Right now, you're rich in ways that you might not have appreciated. You're following your dream, you're creating a business from scratch, you're embarking on a new adventure, and you're challenging yourself in ways you might not have thought possible. Think about what you feel rich in right now, and focus on that when you start feeling discouraged.

I found it helpful to read the daily essays in *Simple Abundance: A Daybook of Comfort and Joy*, by Sarah Ban Breathnach. This may be a bit New Age-y for your taste, but try to find something that helps you focus on wealth beyond the bottom line.

This habit of thinking expansively keeps you focused on what's possible throughout your business life (and your personal life, for that matter). For example, when you're negotiating with a client about a budget, you could choose to approach it as a zero-sum game or you could decide instead to be entirely transparent and work with your client to achieve a goal you both want.

This is a conversation I had with a client who was interested in bringing me into her company for some professional development.

Client: So, before we go any farther, how much will it cost me to have you develop a program?

Me: A lot depends on what would work best for you and how in-depth you see this. Do you have a rough budget for this?

Client: Um, shouldn't you be telling me your proposed budget?

Me: Once I know how much you have in mind, I'll have a much better idea of what would work best for you and how you can get the most value for your budget. We might want to do a half-day workshop, a follow-up webinar in a month, maybe some short e-books on the key areas, and of course I'm available for six months of e-mail support. Knowing how much you want to spend will help me create a plan that will have a lot of impact.

Client: Oh, I see. Well, we have $8,000 we can spend now and we can extend the contract into the next fiscal year if we need to.

With this information, I was able to structure a proposal that was within her budget and that would measurably improve her staff's skills. I didn't waste time sending her a proposal with various price points and options that were clearly not appropriate for her budget. And she got a workshop and the follow-up support that she needed, without paying for anything she didn't think would be useful.

You can find opportunities everywhere to change your perspective by thinking more abundantly. Say you want to attend a conference and don't think you can afford it. Expansive thinking can help you identify other ways of funding your trip. You could offer to work at the registration desk and provide behind-the-scenes support in exchange for your registration. You could inquire about grants and scholarships available through an association, local nonprofit, or the Small Business Administration. If you have writing skills, you could find a publication that would value an article covering the key points of the conference; you can get a press pass to attend the event, get paid to write about it, and get publicity from your article.

Is It Important or Is It Just Urgent?

Most entrepreneurs don't have the luxury of an assistant who can take care of all of their pesky to-do items. Over the course of a day, you may feel pulled in many directions, and your attention may be drawn by whatever has the shortest deadline. You open your e-mail inbox and see ten new messages, some of which are flagged as urgent. You have a voicemail message from a prospective client. A colleague texts you to ask if you can take a few minutes to go over his slide deck. And you have a client project due in a week that you need to start. It's tempting to focus on tasks that can be done quickly and that "must" be done soon, rather than stepping back and looking at the bigger picture.

After a few too many days in which I was busy but not particularly productive, I have learned to be ruthless about how I spend my time. Instead of being driven by whatever appears to be the biggest crisis, my goal now is to focus on what matters the most and to set my priorities based on what I really want to accomplish. So here's how I address the conflicting demands of my time and discern between the truly important and the temporarily urgent.

- E-mail

  I open my e-mail twice a day—generally late morning and then mid-afternoon. I allot a set amount of time to spend on e-mail and I actually set a timer so that I stay on track. Any e-mail that requires more than two or three minutes gets moved into a project folder to be addressed later.

- Texts

  If it would take me more than a minute to answer a text, I send a response that I'm in the middle of something and will get back within a few hours. When I have a break between other tasks, I answer any pending texts.

- Unexpected requests

  Like many entrepreneurs, I like to say yes. If I am asked a favor that interrupts my work flow, I can now say, "I don't have time to focus on that right now. If I can work on it next week, I would be happy to do it. If you need it before then, I can't help you this time."

- Ongoing projects

  I admit, sometimes it's tempting to put off a project until just before the deadline and then slam it out in a rush of adrenalin. A more satisfying, although perhaps less thrilling, approach involves scheduling time every day on each ongoing project. By avoiding my last-minute frenzy, I find that I free up time to devote to some of those unexpected requests.

One big test of your ability to think expansively is whether and how you give yourself time off. Yes, you will go on vacation—or you'll go bonkers. Some entrepreneurs like to tack on a few vacation days at the end of a business trip or attendance at a professional conference. I find that difficult, on several levels. On a practical level, it means I have to pack two wardrobes—one for business and one for play—which doubles the luggage. I also tend to go into marketing overdrive while I'm at a conference, and it's hard for me to switch from business professional to tourist overnight. Finally, by the end of a business trip, I'm ready to get back in the office and get caught up with e-mail and backlogged work, not kick back and chill for a few days.

On the other hand, these mini-vacations can be a nice way to get a few days of relaxation without the hassle of planning a separate trip. You've already written off the travel costs as a business expense, so your only nondeductible expenses are the extra days of hotel and food. And, let's face it, professional conferences are often held at nice destinations.

If nothing else, schedule yourself one day once a month to play hooky from work. Close your e-mail and turn your phone off. Yes, really. Do something that replenishes you—visit a museum, spend the afternoon in a park, read a trashy novel, take photographs—whatever gets you away from the siren call of your office. You'll find that you have a better attitude about the occasional 12-hour day if you know that it enables you to take a break when you want one.

When a Nine-to-Five Job Looks Tempting

Many entrepreneurs occasionally yearn for the (perceived) stability of a regular job, where they show up five days a week and get paid every two weeks. Maybe it's during a time when you're experiencing a client drought, or perhaps when you're working far too many hours for what you're getting paid. You find yourself over at CareerBuilder.com or Monster.com, browsing through job ads.

I consider this a symptom of a need to commit. My spouse often uses the analogy with her clients of being "in the pool or out of the pool." Either you're willing to jump in and swim or you'll sit and dangle your legs over the edge, unwilling to fully engage.

To extend this analogy, looking through job listings while you're running a business is like being in the pool but still hanging on to the ladder. Yes, you're in—but you're never going to actually swim until you let go of that ladder. It will still be there if you decide you can't swim anymore; your focus needs to be on swimming in the pool.

If you feel yourself succumbing to the apparent allure of becoming an employee, think about what it is that you don't like about your business right now. Rather than divide your focus and energy between finding a job and building a business, choose which avenue you want to pursue wholeheartedly. Entrepreneurs who are considering traditional employment often mention the following concerns. See if any of these sounds familiar to you, and consider your options for refocusing on what you really want to do.

- Are you scared because you don't have enough (or any!) clients?
  A lack of clients simply means that you haven't yet figured out what your clients most value and how to effectively communicate your expertise. If your current marketing approach isn't working, you need to conduct some research to find out what your clients really want and how they describe their most pressing needs. Chapter 4, *Who Are Your Clients?*, walks you through the steps involved.

- Are you unable to cover all your overhead expenses?
  The financial realities of being self-employed have hit you. You suddenly find that you have to pay the employer's portion of your Social Security (FICA) taxes; you are now charged the full cost of your health insurance payments. Chapter 7, *All About Money*, describes how you set your billing rate at a level that ensures you can pay for the additional overhead of self-employment. Also see the sidebar "The Health Insurance Puzzle" for more on this rapidly-changing issue.

- Do you miss the stability of a regular paycheck?
  First, remember that no employment is guaranteed. Instead of relying on one employer for all of your income, you're building a base of multiple "employers" (we call them clients). And if you want to reduce your cash flow fluctuations, explore ways to create ongoing relationships with multiple clients. What can you provide every month that your clients value and that they can't get anywhere else?

- Do you miss the atmosphere of the office and the presence of colleagues?
  Some entrepreneurs get their fix of office buzz by working on their projects in coffee shops and other busy venues. They appreciate the stimulation while still being able to go back to their quiet home office after a couple of hours of noise and activity. Other entrepreneurs seek out local networking groups and other face-to-face meetings where they can interact with other people on a regular basis.

Being an entrepreneur means getting a daily reminder of your strengths and weaknesses. You regularly push yourself beyond your comfort zone. Your business continually evolves as you learn how you can provide the highest value for your clients. You'll always be learning new skills to better serve your clients' needs. And you'll always be challenging yourself in new ways, some of which may have you reaching for the ladder to get out of the pool. Take a few deep breaths and decide if you want to climb out of the pool or push yourself off the side and into the deep end.

The Health Insurance Puzzle

One of the reasons people give for staying in jobs they hate—at least in the United States—is their fear of losing their health insurance. It's true that being an entrepreneur means covering the cost of insurance and, if you aren't already covered by your spouse, you'll need to buy individual coverage. The roll-out of Obamacare has meant that individuals have more options for health insurance; you may also be eligible for group health insurance through a professional association or other membership group.

The best place to start investigating your health insurance options is healthcare.gov, where you can view the plans available and sign up. Your state's insurance commission may have additional information on programs and subsidies available to residents. The National Association of Insurance Commissioners has a map with links to each state's insurance department at www.naic.org/state_web_map.htm.

From my own experience of being self-employed for more than twenty years, I've found that the cost of health insurance doesn't need to be the insurmountable obstacle it often appears to those still covered by their employer. Depending on your overall health, age, and desired level of coverage, you may need to pay what seems like a large amount for your health insurance. I view this as a small price to pay for the freedom I get as an entrepreneur.

Business Coaches: Help, I Need Somebody

If you have issues to work out in your personal life, you might see a therapist or counselor. If you need help working out business issues, a business coach could be a godsend. Jan Davis of Blue Sage Research has worked with a business coach and described her experience this way:

Business coaches get into the psychology of running a business—the personal baggage we may bring to the business as well as the issues of running our business in sync with our personal goals and values. They hold us accountable for the priorities we set, such as taking time off, raising rates, and saying no. I found the experience of having a monthly phone conversation with a business coach very worthwhile. Like therapy, there were things I learned about myself that I didn't necessarily like but that I needed to change in order to run a business harmoniously. Having a business coach really is like having a business therapist.

Business coaches aren't mentors in the sense of unpaid guides or advisors. Rather, they're professionals with expertise and skill in helping people identify and think through the things that are keeping them from achieving their full professional potential. Finding a business coach is often a matter of word of mouth, asking colleagues whom they would recommend. Note that I offer strategic business coaching services for both new and long-time entrepreneurs. You can find more information about my coaching services at batesinfo.com/coaching.

Five Self-Management Tips

- Focus on wealth beyond the bottom line.
- Your success is dependent on your ability to make—and learn from—lots of mistakes.

- Unstructured time is difficult for some entrepreneurs; be mindful of how you spend your day.
- You can find more opportunities when you think more abundantly.
- Be open to new ideas, in whatever context they appear.

7 All About Money

"Curiouser and curiouser!" cried Alice.

LEWIS CARROLL, FROM *ALICE'S ADVENTURES IN WONDERLAND*

While most entrepreneurs start our own businesses because we love the work, love the independence, and love the challenge, we also do it because we have bills to pay and food to put on the table. It's important to develop a comfortable relationship with money, since getting paid and spending money are both critical components of being in business.

Financing Your Business

Regardless of the specific services you provide, you'll have some expenses related to starting up. You'll need a computer—no, you can't run your business off an iPad or smart phone—although you probably don't need any high-end hardware. The exception to my philosophy of K.I.S.S. (Keep It Simple, Stupid) when it comes to technology is this: If your business requires heavy computing power, such as working with multimedia, your IT budget will be higher than average.

You'll probably also want a fast Internet connection, a web site, a logo and other corporate branding, business cards, a professional photo, and other marketing-related items. (For more discussion of marketing, see Chapter 10, *Brand "You."*) Depending on your business, this can amount to several thousand dollars—probably more than you have sitting around in your checking account.

You have several options for funding your business. The simplest and most typical is to pay for it out of your savings. If you're still working as an employee and you're thinking about starting a business, set up a separate savings account now and plan to put $500 in it every month. That may mean eliminating some discretionary spending, but it also means that you can start your business without the burden of debt.

Another option is to write a thorough business plan (see the section "Business Plans and Other Pipe Dreams" in Chapter 5, *Building the Framework*) and present it to selected family members and friends. Ask them to lend you a portion of what you need, at an interest rate equivalent to what they would earn from the bank on a certificate of deposit, and for a period of, say, five years. Of course, you'll treat this loan as one that absolutely must be paid off as promised—the last thing you want to do is lose a friend over a business debt.

Also, local banks may be willing to lend you money, provided you can demonstrate that you have a sound business proposal. Note that most lending organizations expect you to invest your savings or personal equity in the business as well. A lender generally won't finance more than 50 percent of your business, which means that you'll have to invest your own money even if you do take out a loan.

The last, and least attractive, option is to put your expenses on a credit card and pay off the debt as you can. Given that the interest rate on credit cards can be at least 18 percent, this offers a quick path to failure. The total cost of an item purchased on a credit card and paid off gradually can easily double, once you factor in what you are paying in interest. If the only way you can finance your business is through credit-card debt, my suggestion would be to hold off on starting your business until you're in a stronger financial situation.

The U.S. Small Business Administration has a discussion about finding startup money on its website (sba.gov). The section on how to write a loan proposal is particularly useful. Keep in mind that writing a formal business plan in order to obtain a loan can be difficult. Most one-person businesses are as unique as their owners, so it's virtually impossible to get reliable numbers on the size of your market or a projection of your sales. To make sure that your financial projections are reasonable, base your estimates on interviews with potential clients as well as conversations with established businesses.

Accounting 101

Fortunately, you don't need to know much about accounting to run your business, as long as you can set up a system that enables you to keep tabs on your income and expenses. Some entrepreneurs keep it really simple—they put all their expenses on one credit card, they deposit all their income into one checking account, and they hand their credit card statements and check register to their accountant at the end of the year. Others build a spreadsheet that allows them to track their income and expenses by category and monitor their cash flow and outstanding invoices. And still other entrepreneurs find that accounting software such as QuickBooks offers the most flexibility and features and is worth the cost and learning curve required.

Whatever accounting option you choose, there are some functions in which all entrepreneurs need to be proficient. These include

- Creating invoices
- Tracking overdue invoices
- Applying payments to invoices
- Tracking bank deposits
- Paying bills
- Reconciling accounts

I am neither a lawyer nor an accountant. Before you set up your business accounting system, I recommend that you consult with a lawyer for the form of your business and an accountant for the details of tracking your business. What I describe here are ideas for keeping a handle on your cash flow; be sure that your accounting system is appropriate for your situation. Even if you plan on doing your own bookkeeping, I encourage you to bring in an accountant or consultant to help you set up your initial accounting system. You'll save time and your sanity if you start out using the income and expense categories that you'll be referencing in your tax filings. If you're a sole proprietor, consult the current IRS Form 1040 and Schedule C and note how the IRS categorizes your expenses and income. If you're an incorporated business, consult Publication 535, *Business Expenses,* for information on what you can deduct. All the forms and publications are at www.irs.gov.

When you are setting up your income and expense categories, think through how you want to track your money. For example, I have separate income categories for coaching, business research, speaking fees, consulting services, and so on. To the IRS, they are all just gross receipts, but I can generate reports in QuickBooks that show me how much of my revenue comes from each type of work, which lets me gauge the effectiveness of my marketing and plan how I invest my time.

Set up a business checking account and savings account in addition to whatever personal bank accounts you already have. Taxing agencies look more favorably on sole proprietors who keep their personal and business money separate, and it's just simpler this way. Note that some banks require proof that you're already in business before they'll open business accounts. Make sure you have your business license or whatever other forms your local jurisdiction requires before you head to your bank or credit union.

Why should you have a business savings account? You need to put money aside regularly for tax payments as well as for new equipment and unplanned expenditures. And as you learn about the inevitable ebb and flow of income, you need to save up enough money to cover your overhead expenses during those months when your income is exceeded by your outgo.

One aspect of running a business that many entrepreneurs do not enjoy is bookkeeping. While it's tempting to simply throw all the receipts in a shoe box for your accountant to sort out at the end of the year, resist the urge. For starters, unless you keep track of your income and expenses on an ongoing basis, you cannot get an accurate idea of how your business is doing, how financially strong it is, where there are problem areas, and so on. And of course, the end of the tax year is probably not a time when you or your accountant want to address this. If you just can't keep up on the day-to-day accounting, bring in a bookkeeper. If you're a sole proprietor, probably all you need is a careful—and entirely trustworthy— person to track your invoices and bills. If you're incorporated, consider using a bookkeeper to manage your monthly reports and payments. Regardless of the form of your business, once your income approaches what you were making before you started your business, consider having an accountant prepare your taxes to ensure you're taking advantage of any tax benefits. An accountant with a strategic perspective can be a great advisor; my accountant advises me annually of what I should do this year to minimize my taxes.

Setting Your Rates

As any long-time consultant can tell you, setting prices is an art as well as a science. It's a combination of covering your costs, ensuring a fair profit, indicating your estimation of your value to your clients, and determining what the market will bear. Your fees will be based on a combination of factors, including the type of work you do, your client base, the going rate both for the industry you're marketing to and for the profession as a whole, and the salary you want to pay yourself.

There are two ways to determine an hourly rate, which you can use as a baseline for calculating your total fee. The first is to just do a gut-check, decide that you're worth, oh, $200 an hour, and go with it. (If you do set your rate this way, you need a healthy amount of self-confidence. If your gut tells you that you are worth $25 an hour, keep reading.)

> *Build your business around clients who value you at the rate you want to be paid.*

If, on the other hand, you prefer to take the analytical approach—or at least be able to justify your fee in your own mind—here's a formula to help you. It takes a little while to work through this process, but you'll end up setting an hourly rate that will sustain you. The theory here is to figure out what you *need* to bring in, in order to cover your costs and earn a satisfactory income. And keep in mind that this is your baseline hourly rate; when you know that you're adding exceptional value or when you know that a lot is at stake, you can adjust your final fee upward to reflect the added value or risk involved.

Salary

Decide what annual salary you want to pay yourself. Be realistic: don't build in a salary so low that you can't make a living, and don't expect to pay yourself $300,000 the first year. Since your clients expect your hourly rate to stay the same over time, resist the urge to start low and then raise your salary later. If you set your rate too low now, you'll be building a business around people who expect you to continue to be low cost. If in a year you want to double your salary, you'll have to increase your hourly rate, which means that you'll have to find a new set of clients willing to pay your higher fee.

Taxes

Calculate what you'll have to pay in taxes. Remember that, since you're now a business, even if just a sole proprietor, you'll have to pay the taxes that your employer would normally pay. If you're unsure, assume that 25 percent or so of your income will go toward your taxes.

Investments

Add in the amount you need to set aside in a year for retirement, children's education, and other long-term financial goals.

Overhead

Next, figure out your non-reimbursable and overhead expenses for a full year. This includes everything except expenses you can bill back directly to clients. It includes just about everything you'll be paying for, such as:

- Office rent, if needed.
- Utilities (phone, Internet service).
- Insurance payments (health, property, liability).
- Office supplies (paper, toner, business cards, stamps, etc.).

- Annual membership dues for professional associations—those your clients are members of and those for your own professional development.
- Travel and registration costs for any relevant and cost-effective professional conferences to market yourself, refresh your skills, and stay on top of your clients' issues and concerns.
- Office equipment—assume that you'll have to replace your phone and your computer every few years, and include the cost of any other equipment you need for your business.
- Accountants' fees, professional magazine and journal subscriptions, and other miscellaneous costs.
- Marketing and advertising expenses—for most entrepreneurs offering a professional service, these costs may not be more than $1,000.

It's hard to estimate all of these overhead items ahead of time; most beginning entrepreneurs can expect to spend between $5,000 and $25,000 in overhead. Variables include whether you want your business to pay for your insurance expenses, how many conferences you attend, and any specialized equipment or training your profession requires.

Billable Time

Now let's figure out how many hours you can bill in a year. It's probably not as many as you think. Start with fifty-two weeks. Subtract at least two weeks for vacation (at least one week of actual vacation and a week of random days when you need to take a "mental health day"). Subtract another week for medical appointments and sick days. Subtract another two to three weeks for non-billable holidays (all the holidays that regular employees get) because, let's face it, you don't want to have to work on Thanksgiving and New Year's Day. And finally, subtract at least one week for unexpected problems. Your basement will flood and you spend two days dealing with it. Or your family pays a visit and wants your undivided attention. Or your spouse breaks both wrists and you need to take over the driving duties for both of you. If you plan for the unexpected, then you won't have to be as concerned about the "lost" time from these unplanned interruptions. You'll probably wind up with around forty-five weeks of time that you can expect to be working.

Instead of constantly having to justify your fees, expand your idea of who your clients are and what you do.

How many hours will you bill each week? For most professionals, the answer is no more than twenty or thirty hours—and that assumes a full forty-hour work week. So once you factor in how many billable weeks there are in a year, you can probably plan on billing no more than 1,000 or 1,500 hours a year, assuming you can generate that much work, week after week.

In addition to doing what your clients are paying you for, you'll spend a significant amount of time marketing, answering e-mail, marketing, preparing for presentations or meetings, marketing, sending out invoices, marketing, paying bills, marketing, and so on. Trust me on this: you'll spend a lot of your time marketing. Even if one major client takes up most of your time, you still need to invest in marketing so that you have other clients when—not if—that client engagement comes to an end. As a general rule, relying on one client for more than 25 or 30 percent of your revenue is dangerous; if you lose that client your income will plummet.

So what do we have? In simple math, it looks like this:

Your annual salary plus taxes plus investments plus overhead
divided by
The number of hours you expect to bill in a year

To illustrate, here's how an event planner might set her hourly rate. She decides that her annual salary will be $50,000. She estimates that her taxes, marketing, and other overhead (expenses that she can't pass along to her clients) will run about $20,000 a year. That means that she needs to bring in at least $70,000 a year to meet her goals.

Based on her interviews with other event planners, she knows to expect to bill no more than twenty-five hours in a forty-hour week and no more than forty-four weeks a year. That means that if she's fully booked with clients, she'll bill no more than 1,100 hours (twenty-five hours x forty-four weeks). In order to have at least $70,000 in revenue to pay her salary and expenses, she needs to charge at least $65 an hour ($70,000 divided by 1,100 hours).

Her annual salary plus taxes plus investments plus overhead:
$70,000
divided by
The number of hours she expects to bill in a year: 1,100
equals **$65/hour**

Many entrepreneurs find that this comes to somewhere between $75 and $200 per hour. That result is how much you have to bill per hour in order to pay your salary and cover your expenses—again, in order to meet your salary needs, you have to be generating enough business to bill all your available hours.

For many beginning entrepreneurs, this rate may sound absurdly high; some others may look at the number and imagine six-figure salaries their first month in business. Reality lies somewhere in between. Since most people don't start their business with clients ready to engage them, it will probably take six months to start bringing in enough income to pay yourself your salary. After you get your marketing momentum going and you learn what your clients value the most, your biggest limitation will be how big you want your business to become.

> *Have a clear agreement with each client about how and when they'll be paying you, and be prepared to follow up if you haven't been paid within the time period you both agreed to.*

If your intended client base is likely to balk at your rate, think long and hard about whether you want to take a substantial pay cut in order to work with this group of clients. Instead of constantly having to justify your fees, consider expanding your idea of who your clients are and what you do. Who else could benefit from your services and has the ability and willingness to pay you for your brilliance and expertise? Go back to Chapter 4, *Who Are Your Clients?*, and reconsider all the possible types of clients you could attract.

Billing and Collections

Unlike employees, who receive a steady paycheck, entrepreneurs get paid only after they've billed their clients and collected the money. In order to maintain at least some semblance of a steady cash flow, it's important to invoice quickly and follow up promptly on any invoices that are past due. Depending on your business and your clients, you may need to require prepayment or payment at the time you provide your product or service.

When you're discussing a job with a client, take time to explicitly discuss payment terms, and listen to the client's response. If the client sounds hesitant or ambiguous, I ask for prepayment or a credit card number that I can charge at the end of the job. Listen to your gut. There are times when, as soon as you bring up the matter of payment, you get a sense that this client just isn't going to pay the bill. If that happens, it's perfectly reasonable for you to require prepayment or to decline the work. I've lost a couple of potential clients who were unwilling to prepay or to trust me with their credit card numbers; since I value the mutual trust and respect that I have with my clients, I knew that they were never going to be a good fit.

Should You Take Credit Cards?

Many entrepreneurs are reluctant to accept payment by credit or debit card, out of concern about security or high processing fees. I encourage businesses to set up an account with a credit card processing service in the interest of making it as easy as possible for your client to pay you. In order to charge a credit or debit card, you need to have what's called a "merchant account" with a bank or through a credit card processing company such as PayPal or Square. Having a merchant account enables you to swipe a credit card with a small device attached to your smart phone or tablet or manually type in the information on a mobile device or laptop. Your transaction is secure and your client's credit card information is safe when you use one of these services.

The amount you charge will be deposited into your account, less a fee that ranges from 2 percent to 4 percent. While those fees can add up, consider it part of your overhead and set your rates with that in mind. I've found that the ability to get paid immediately, less 4 percent, is often better than waiting sixty or ninety days for the full payment.

If you're working on a project with a client that will take weeks or months to complete, build in interim milestones and partial payment terms. If your client ever gets behind on payments, you have the option to stop working until you've been paid; my approach has been to assume that if a client really needs me for a large project, they'll find a way to ensure that I'm paid on time.

Net 30 Means Net 30

When you get a bill from the utility company, it usually includes the date by which you're expected to pay. In the business world, this is often written as "net 30" or "net 15." Net 30 means that you're expected to pay the net total amount owned—that is, the total after taking into account any credits or refunds—within thirty days of the date of the invoice. Net 30 is typical, but other payment terms exist. If you want to be paid for the time you provide a service, or when you present an invoice, make that clear with your client before you begin work.

It's important to stay on top of your receivables, being mindful that different clients will have different payment patterns and methods. Some can easily write you a check at the time you provide the service. Others will require that you register with their accounts payable department, submit an invoice, and wait sixty days for them to send you the money. Make sure that you have a clear agreement with each client about how and when they'll be paying you, and be prepared to follow up if you haven't been paid within the time period you both agreed to.

Your accounting software can generate past-due reports that show you which invoices haven't been paid on time. I usually give my client a few days after the thirty-day mark because I've found that some companies have a policy of mailing the check the day it is due. If your clients are large corporations and you get to a week beyond the due date, call the client's accounts payable office to confirm that they received the invoice and to check whether they need any additional information. Most accounting departments require an IRS Form W-9, which provides them with your Employer Identification Number. (For more discussion about using an EIN for your business rather than your Social Security number, see Chapter 5, *Building the Framework*.) If you include a copy of your W-9 with every invoice, you may speed up the payment process.

If you have a client who is habitually slow to pay, you may want to require prepayment before you begin work on the next job, or agree that you'll charge the client's credit card when payment is due. There's no reason for you to act as a short-term lender for clients who have trouble managing their cash flow.

If you're dealing with a small organization, there's probably one person handling all the company's bills. If so, get to know that person, who is going to be your new best friend. Ask him what he needs to process your invoice smoothly. Enclose a self-addressed stamped envelope. I'm on a first-name basis with the accounting people of several of my clients, and my invoices always get paid promptly.

On the other hand, be mindful of the limitations of a large organization. You may be one of hundreds of vendors, and their accounts payable department's policy may be to cut checks forty-five days after the date of the invoice. You can complain all you want, but they won't change their procedure for one relatively small vendor. If necessary, build an annoyance factor into your price and resign yourself to waiting forty-five days for payment. My philosophy is that it's better to wait an additional fifteen days than become a source of irritation to my client.

Deadbeats and Other "Learning Opportunities"

In the ideal world, if you ensure that you have prepayment or a credit card from every new client, and if you maintain a good relationship with your clients, you shouldn't encounter problems getting paid. Unfortunately, in the real world there are people who seem nice but who choose not to pay for your services. First, remember that you should never take a risk with a new client; even if she was referred to you by your brother-in-law, get a credit card or prepayment. (My accountant has agreed to be the fall guy for this. If I get resistance to this request, I say, "Oh, my accountant is just a tyrant about this. She insists that I get a credit card or prepayment from every new client.")

However, there may come a time that a repeat client refuses to pay an invoice, or you forget to request prepayment or a credit card number from a new client. This has happened to me three times over the course of two decades of business. In my experience, these situations are not matters in which a faceless accounts payable department is sitting on your invoice; these are almost always cases of an individual consultant or business owner refusing to pay. Hence, your collection efforts will probably be directed at your client, not an accounting department.

These are the steps I have taken, in escalating order.

- Keep a paper trail of everything.
  If you have a phone conversation asking about the status of payment, follow up with an e-mail—"as we discussed today . . ."—outlining what was said. You want to be able to say, "When I called you last week, you told me that you were writing a check that day. I haven't received it yet. Would it be easier for you to give me your credit card number to take care of this?" If nothing else, you have a record of how

many times, and over what period of time, you have tried to collect on the invoice.

- Set up a separate e-mail address.
  If you can set up a second e-mail address with your business domain name, send one more e-mail, this time from accounting@your-company.com. Spell out the amount due, your efforts to collect, and a deadline for payment.
- Have your lawyer draft a letter requesting payment.
  Sometimes this is sufficient to get the attention of a slow-paying client. If the client is in your local area, you can consider taking him to court. However, the time and energy involved in this will probably exceed the value of the money you're recouping.
- Finally, if it's clear that you're not going to get paid, forgive the debt.
  My philosophy is that bad clients don't deserve any more of my energy or focus. I wait until the debt is six or nine months old and then write off the amount owed. I send the client a letter to that effect; it usually includes wording such as this: "I'm sorry that you are unable to pay for the work that I did for you in April. It's clear to me that you do not intend to honor this invoice, so I'm forgiving the debt. I trust that in your business dealings, your clients respect your time and expertise more than you have respected mine." This has the effect of removing the source of irritation from my life, and I release that energy-drain from my business. I know that, when it comes right down to it, it will not be cost-effective in terms of time, money, and energy to pursue payment from a client. I would much rather move on and focus on my good clients.

And, believe it or not, two of my three deadbeats eventually paid me the full amount owed, albeit a year late. Since I had removed the debt from my brain as well as my books, each payment felt like an unexpected gift.

Cash Flow

I remember a character named Wimpy in the old Popeye cartoons I watched as a child. He struggled with cash flow, shall we say, and his refrain was, "I will gladly pay you Tuesday for a hamburger today."

During your first couple of years in business, you may feel a bit like Wimpy. The phone bill comes in and has to be paid, regardless of whether you have been paid by your last client. Get in the habit of banking every client payment rather than immediately spending it. You don't know yet when your business's peaks and valleys will occur, and you need enough money in the bank to pay the bills.

Watch your overhead expenses—the costs you incur independent of how much work you're doing and how much income you expect. Particularly when you start your business, think long and hard about any potential expense that isn't directly related to gaining new clients or providing billable information services to existing clients. After you've been in business a year or two, you can think about buying that high-end tech gadget; until then, keep your overhead to a minimum while investing strategically where it will help you expand your business.

Keep track of when bills are due and make sure that you pay your vendors on time. Your credit rating is a valuable asset and, once lost, is difficult to restore. If you think you're going to be late in making a payment, call the vendor immediately, explain the situation, and see if you can negotiate a better payment option. You don't want your phone line to go dead or your e-mail address to disappear because you didn't pay your bills promptly. Your clients will be inclined to shop elsewhere if they have trouble getting in touch with you.

There are lots of ways to get the most from your accounts payable and accounts receivable in order to maximize your cash flow. These are a few techniques that can work well for entrepreneurs.

Money Coming In

- Offer a discount for full prepayment of your fee (5 to 10 percent is reasonable).
- Accept credit card payments. This can significantly speed payment.
- Always discuss payment at the beginning of the project; ensure that your client agrees to pay you within thirty days.

Money Going Out

- When possible, pay your invoices with a credit card, but only if you'll be able to pay it off in full when the bill arrives. This allows you to postpone payment until a client's check arrives.
- Eliminate finance charges and late fees. Pay off any interest-incurring debt as soon as possible.
- Whenever you can, ask, "Is that the best rate you can give me?" rather than "What discounts do I qualify for?"

Even if a bookkeeper routinely manages your invoices and payments, you should monitor your cash flow weekly. Know how much money you have available, what bills are coming due, and when you can expect to receive payment from clients.

And finally, I will lapse into my coaching personality and encourage you to view your business with abundance. They call it cash "flow" because it flows—in and out. Think of what happens when you put a kink in a hose—the water stops flowing. Look at the money that comes into and out of your business as being part of a flow. If you feel constricted and afraid, you kink the hose. If you act from a perspective of expansion, the money often seems to flow in more easily, too. I give money to several nonprofits whether or not I think I can spare it, on the assumption that this keeps the energetic flow of money going. And sure enough, it always seems to. When I can feel (responsibly) generous with my finances, I make decisions from a bigger, more expansive place, and I have yet to regret any of those decisions.

Paying the Tax Man

Unless you've incorporated your business, you're no longer a payroll employee; no one is withholding the IRS's take on your behalf. Four times a year, even before they ask for it (yes, I know it's painful), you'll pay the IRS a percentage of your estimated total income tax for the year using IRS Form 1040-ES. For more detail, consult IRS Publication 505, *Tax Withholding and Estimated Tax*.

And how do you know what your total income tax liability will be when you're just starting your business? After you've been in business a year, it's pretty easy. The IRS lets you base your quarterly payments on the prior year's total tax liability. Note, however, that tax laws change all the time, and if you expect your revenue this year to be significantly larger than last year's, consult a tax advisor.

All well and good, but what about the first year you're in business? Ask colleagues who went through a similar start-up what you might expect to spend, talk with an accountant, and then make a reasonable guess. Revisit your business plan as the year progresses and make any necessary adjustments in your cash-flow projections. And remember to make those quarterly payments! Note that if your state has an income tax, you must send quarterly estimated tax payments to the state revenue office as well.

Be sure you keep careful receipts for and records of all your business expenses. And keep in mind that your definition of a "business expense" has to match that of the IRS. Sole proprietors and small businesses seem to be disproportionately targeted for audits, and you want to be sure that you have documentation for anything you claim as a business expense. The IRS offers a fairly clear description of what constitutes a business expense for a small business or self-employed individual in Publication 535, *Business Expenses*, which you can download from www.irs.gov. The short answer to "What is a business expense?" is this: the expense is for something ordinary and necessary in your industry—in other words, it has to pass the straight-face test. You can often tack a vacation onto the end of a business trip, for example, but you cannot write off the entire expense of your housecleaning service if your office occupies one room of your house. And, though your health club membership keeps you fit and alert, it is not a legitimate business write-off. Much to my regret as a frequent flier, neither are airport lounge memberships.

Five Financial Tips

- Watch out for unnecessary overhead expenses and recurring costs.
- Consider requiring prepayment from clients, particularly for large projects.
- Learn to be comfortable talking about payment terms with clients.
- Stay on top of your receivables.
- Monitor your cash flow.

8 The Care and Feeding of Clients

> [The White Rabbit] came trotting along in a great hurry,
> muttering to himself, as he came,
> "Oh! The Duchess, the Duchess! Oh!
> Wo'n't she be savage if I've kept her waiting!"

LEWIS CARROLL, FROM *ALICE'S ADVENTURES IN WONDERLAND*

Clients are strange creatures; sometimes we love them and sometimes they drive us crazy. If you didn't have clients, you'd be out of business, but how do you manage their expectations, keep them happy, *and* handle those occasional situations in which everything seems to go wrong?

You're the Boss

As a one-person business, *you* are your company in your clients' eyes, even if you have other people working with you on projects. This means that you're responsible for how satisfied a client is with your services. Yes, there are unreasonable people in the world, and a few of them may become your clients. How you handle difficult or challenging situations with your clients is determined to some extent by what psychologists call "locus of control." Do you believe that what happens to you is primarily due to your own actions, or do you often think that you have no control over what happens in your life? People with an internal locus of control tend to assume that they determine their own future, and people with an external locus of control often believe that what happens to them is the result of luck or external factors they cannot control.

> *Entrepreneurs can look at their business dispassionately,*
> *decide that their current approach isn't working,*
> *and shift their focus to something that would be*
> *more successful and more fun.*

Entrepreneurs with a healthy internal locus of control see their business as something they create themselves. They maintain warm relationships with their clients without personalizing the occasional glitch. They can look at their business dispassionately and decide that, as it turns out, their current approach isn't working and they can shift their focus to something that would be more successful and more fun.

Here are some examples of the differences between external and internal loci of control.

External: "I had no choice."
Internal: "I didn't look at all the alternatives."

External: "She makes me so mad!"
Internal: "I am choosing to react angrily to her."

External: "I can't . . ." or "If only . . ."
Internal: "What do I need to do in order to . . . ?"

External: "My clients won't let me . . ."
Internal: "I haven't yet successfully negotiated with my clients about . . ."

External: "People take advantage of me."
Internal: "Thanks for asking; I just can't do that right now."

Thinking Bigger

How do you describe yourself when someone asks you what you do? Given my background as a corporate librarian, I used to talk about how I *help* my clients. Depending on the context, I might describe my business as helping reluctant entrepreneurs build their business, or helping clients understand their competitive environment, or helping companies communicate better with their clients.

I eventually realized that describing myself as a helper downplayed my role as a creative problem-solver and strategic thinker. Clients don't usually sit up one day and think, "Wow, I need help! I'd better call Mary Ellen!" Rather, they find themselves in a situation they want to change, and they remember that I have an expertise they can use to make changes.

I began looking at myself in a larger context, challenging myself to be as big and creative as I wanted to be (gulp!). I shifted my perspective when I was approaching a project and began asking myself what else I could do and how else I could do it. My questions included these:

- What is the underlying problem or need (or interest) here? What brings my client to me?
- How can I offer an outcome with even more impact? What does my client not even know I can do?
- What else does my client need? What else would delight my client?
- What would help my client be able to say "yes"? Does my client need to get approval for this project? What can I provide that would make clear the value I offer?

When you're just starting your business, shifting your perspective may feel like a stretch. You don't have any clients and, truth to tell, you would take just about any offer to create income. Think bigger!

Tire-Kickers, Lookie-Loos, and Low-Ballers

We all know what tire-kickers are—they're the people who wander through the used car lot, kicking tires and tying up a salesperson's time without intending to actually buy a car. "Lookie-loo" is the name real estate agents give to the folks who love to wander through open houses and look around but who have no interest in buying real estate. And low-ballers are the clients who always work on getting a "better deal"—who try to negotiate the budget down for every project and get the most they can from you for less than you want to charge.

> *A client who only hires you because you're cheap will be gone as soon as he finds someone cheaper.*

I can almost guarantee that you'll get a phone call from one of these characters soon after you start your business. They'll talk and talk and talk, they'll ask you all about your services and imply that they are just about to buy . . . but they have to shop around a bit first to see if you have the lowest price in town. Your challenge is figuring out how to get off the phone gracefully without offending the caller or spending too much time with someone who isn't going to become a sustainable client.

My solution is to watch the clock. I have gotten into the habit of noting the time at the beginning of a phone call. If we haven't gotten down to talking about the details of the job and the budget within five or ten minutes, I bring up the issue. Depending on the situation, I will ask:

- What's your rough budget for this?
- How much do you have in mind to spend?
- This is my usual hourly rate; most projects like this take about ten hours. Will that work with your budget?

These questions offer respectful ways to learn the size and scope of my client's expectations, which helps me know whether I'm a good match for this client, and a nice way to let the lookie-loos know that I'm going to start talking about prices.

How do you deal with someone who's shopping around for the lowest bidder? Easy—bid high. Seriously, a client who only hires you because you're cheap will be gone as soon as he finds someone cheaper. If the caller tells you, or implies, that he's comparing you with others to find the lowest price, you may wish to end the conversation right there. My usual response is, "It sounds like you've already identified several excellent companies. I probably don't have the lowest rate, and I price myself according to my value. If you're looking for someone with a lower price, I recommend you go with one of the people you've already called."

Of course, in some lines of work it's customary to ask for competing bids, and the buyer compares the budget as well as the expertise of each company, their ability to handle the work, personal recommendations, and so on. When I needed to sell my house, I asked several real estate brokers for proposals. On the other hand, when I needed to find an accountant, I asked my network of local entrepreneurs, interviewed one who came well-recommended, and have been a happy client ever since. I had no need to shop around and compare accountants because I had asked for referrals from people who had similar needs and concerns, so I was more concerned with making sure the accountant and I communicated well.

The Job from Hell

As a lifelong dog owner (an aside: here in Boulder we are referred to as "animal guardians"), I know that there are no bad dogs, just bad matches between a dog and its person. Similarly, I have learned that there are few truly bad clients . . . just situations that didn't work out. These usually arise from some combination of miscommunication, my lack of managing expectations, and my not speaking up as soon as a glitch appeared.

There are some projects that spell trouble from the start:

- Your client says or implies that she won't pay you if the final result isn't exactly what she expected.
- The project requires that you become proficient in an area in which you have no prior experience or familiarity.
- Your client is not clear about what he wants, and he suggests that the scope of the project may shift as you go forward.
- You're unclear on the scope and depth of the project and can't get further clarity from your client.

What happens if you find yourself in one of these situations and you don't address and resolve it immediately? The client becomes angry because he didn't get what he expected, or he thinks the bill is excessive, or he wants you to do far more than what you thought you had agreed to. You can wind up embroiled in the Project from Hell.

The one thing *not* to do in a situation like this is argue. Your client is already unhappy/anxious/ impatient/frustrated/fill-in-the-blank. If you get an irate phone call or e-mail, try to put yourself in the client's shoes before getting defensive. At the moment, it doesn't really matter what happened; what your client wants to hear is that you care and that you will make it better.

What *not* to say in this situation:

- "This has never happened before!"
- "Sorry, no refunds."
- "But I did just what you asked for. What's your problem?"
- "Well, as soon as you pay my invoice, we can talk about what else I can do for you."

What you *can* say to defuse the situation:

- "I feel terrible that this happened. What can we do now to get back on track?"
- "I am so sorry that this wasn't what you expected; let's talk about what our options are now."
- "What can I do to make this better?"

> *It's your responsibility to recognize and watch for pitfalls and address your client's problems before they become unsolvable.*

Note that you don't necessarily have to admit fault—although, of course, if the problem was your fault, or due to a misunderstanding or faulty assumption that might well have been yours, you should say so. The object is to demonstrate to your client that you can see the situation from her perspective. Later, when you've both calmed down, you can figure out where and why the miscommunication happened.

Maybe you didn't explain to the client that she might not get exactly what she wanted, or the two of you didn't come to an understanding on the parameters of the project, or you didn't alert her early in the process that her initial expectations weren't reasonable, or you took on a project that you didn't fully understand, or your client simply didn't accept the limitations of the time frame and budget, or you didn't listen to your gut when it said, "Walk away from this one—it's a loser."

You might notice a pattern here; just about all the possible reasons for a project going bad include you as one of the factors. That doesn't mean that the customer is always right; in fact, the client may be clinically delusional. But it's your responsibility to recognize and watch for those pitfalls and address problems before they become unsolvable—by taking more time to discuss and manage the client's expectations, by articulating the limits on what you can and will do within the client's budget, and by walking away from a job that you don't think you could do splendidly. Of course, this assumes that you keep your part of the bargain—you do deliver what you promised, on time and within budget. And what if you can't? You pick up the phone as soon as you realize that there's going to be a problem and you negotiate, with the understanding that this is *your* problem and the client is under no obligation to let you off the hook. Your job is to take responsibility for any project that goes bad, without needing to beat yourself up for the part you played.

What do you do if, despite your best efforts, your client isn't happy with the results of your work or services? Up to a certain point, it makes sense to absorb the cost, at least for the portion of your invoice that covers your time as distinguished from any direct expenses. See what additional work you can do to make the client happy, and don't bill the additional time. Call it a learning experience.

Remember that a client you treat respectfully will probably call you again. I have several long-time clients with whom I have occasionally experienced miscommunications. I have always apologized, expressed my mortification that this misunderstanding happened, and either not billed them for the job or charged them only for my out-of-pocket costs. They have always returned with more work; I have demonstrated that I want their business and am willing to give them the benefit of the doubt. Up to a certain point, it's a good investment to let one invoice go if it's likely that the client will call you again.

Of course, you must see how the client behaves in the future. If you sense as you start to negotiate the next project that you're going to have problems again, you might want to politely turn down the work and refer the client to someone else.

Fishing for Feedback

We all like hearing compliments, and very few people actively solicit criticism. On the other hand, nothing is more frustrating to a business owner than a client who is unhappy with the work and, instead of giving the business owner a chance to rectify the problem, simply takes his business elsewhere. We can't resolve a problem unless we hear about it, and—human nature being what it is—people are often reluctant to complain about service directly to the person involved. If you aren't pleased with your web designer, aren't you more inclined to simply move your business elsewhere than to call her up and tell her how annoyed you are when she doesn't return phone calls promptly or has a too-brusque manner?

Our challenge as business owners is to actively encourage these complaints. If you feel queasy at the thought of eliciting criticism, think about similar situations in your personal life. We've all had experiences where a product or service was quite unsatisfactory, but the company was so responsive in rectifying the problem that we were left with a positive impression at the end. Everyone understands that life happens and that sometimes we make mistakes. The critical point is the next step—identifying the problem and fixing it by bringing the end result up to the expected level of quality.

How you reach out to solicit feedback will depend on your business and your clients. You can call, e-mail, or text your clients a few days after you finish each project to see if they have any questions or concerns. If you haven't heard from a client in a while, check in to find out what's new and see if you're still on their radar.

How to Fire a Client

Wait—you're supposed to *find* clients, not fire them, right? In general, that is true, but one of the perks of running your own business is that you can gracefully get rid of clients with whom you just don't want to work anymore. It's always a hard decision; you hate to lose the income from a client. On the other hand, being an entrepreneur means having to manage yourself, your time, and your energy. If a client becomes a burden to you—financially, mentally, or emotionally—it could be time to let him go.

When should you think about firing a client or, at the least, helping a client find someone else who can better handle his unique needs?

- If you feel angry or anxious whenever the client calls
- If working for the client is significantly more time consuming and less profitable than doing similar jobs for other clients
- If the client is consistently verbally abusive, offensive, rude, or demanding
- If the client routinely complains about your rates
- If the client habitually pays your invoices later than agreed
- If the client pressures you to do something that you believe is unethical or illegal

Even though it is tempting to simply call the client and yell, "I'm never going to work for you again!" this is probably not the wisest approach. Life is too short for unproductive arguments, and nothing fruitful comes from an angry interaction. And, in most situations, the softer path is just as effective and far easier.

Think back to high school. When you were dating and wanted to break up, the standard line was, "It's not you, it's me. I'm just not right for you." Take that sentiment, tune it to the adult world, and it really can work. You can tell the client that her projects are falling outside your area of expertise or that you're becoming so busy with other work that you can no longer fulfill her requests within her deadlines. And if the client doesn't believe you, turn down her next request, using whatever reason you gave her—you simply can't meet the deadline or you just couldn't take on the request because it goes outside your realm of expertise. Yes, it takes nerves of steel to turn down work this way, but you can do it. If appropriate, refer the client to a colleague or to a directory of others who are in your line of work. Just because the client didn't work well with you does not mean that someone else cannot handle her.

Before you fire a client, though, ask yourself what you're really angry about. Lynn Peterson, of PFC Information Services, told me about a particularly bad experience when she was about to tell a client that she would no longer work for him.

First, I took a deep breath and asked myself how this situation had come about. I realized that I had let my client talk me into doing far more work than I could do in the time allotted and that I was really just mad at myself for letting this happen. I talked with my client and now he knows what is realistic to expect. This was just a bad situation, not a bad client.

Five Tips for Managing Clients

- See yourself as a valued resource for your clients, not just a freelancer.
- Watch for creative ways to solve your clients' problems.
- Turn down projects or fire clients if the chemistry isn't there.
- Accept responsibility when a project goes bad.
- Demonstrate to your clients that you want and value their business.

9 Your (Fabulous) Marketing Plan

Alice: Who's to say what is "proper"? What if it was agreed
that "proper" was wearing a codfish on your head?
Would you wear it?

FROM *ALICE IN WONDERLAND* (TIM BURTON FILM, 2010)

Many people who go into business for themselves start out by
setting up a web site, ordering business cards, and designing
brochures—all without having first thought through why they're
doing it. But before you can start blogging or sending out
postcards, you need a roadmap to guide you. What's the point
of your blog? What do you want to accomplish with your web
site? How will you know if it was worthwhile sending out those
postcards?

This is where a marketing plan comes in. When you start
your business, you might write a business plan, and while a
business plan can be useful, you will spend most of your time
and energy with a marketing plan, particularly during your first
few years. Similar to a business plan, your marketing plan is a
living document. You write your first one with certain
assumptions and hunches. Over time, your business changes,

your client base evolves, the market morphs, and you identify ways you can more effectively use the available media tools to engage your clients. As you continue to adjust your marketing plan so that it's more effective and more fun, you'll come to appreciate how it keeps you focused on your long-term goals.

> *To achieve your strategic goals for the year,*
> *plan backward instead of forward.*

A marketing plan doesn't need to be a formal document with headings, subheadings, footnotes, and appendixes. However, it does have to provide you with a framework within which to think about how you'll attract and cultivate your clients. Many people find it difficult to think through their marketing strategy before they launch their business, but it's even more difficult to generate business if you don't have a plan and measurable goals for gauging the success of each of your marketing approaches. (Yes, you always have several marketing efforts going simultaneously.)

Lots of books and web sites offer business-plan templates, but fewer relevant sources exist to help you develop a marketing plan that's appropriate for a one-person business. You probably won't be relying on storefront displays, advertising, or a trained sales force to generate business, so most of the techniques in generic plans are not particularly helpful. Instead, design a marketing plan that feels right for you, and consider it a work in progress. You'll modify it as you learn what works and what doesn't work for your particular business and client base. In fact, I review my marketing plan once a month to see what activities I should schedule for the upcoming month and to decide whether I need to alter any of my marketing efforts for the rest of the year.

What Are Your Goals?

It's hard to know you've arrived if you don't have a destination in mind. Likewise, business goals for the year will guide your marketing activities and enable you to track the impact and effectiveness of your various marketing efforts.

To achieve your strategic goals for the year, plan backward instead of forward. That sounds non-intuitive, doesn't it? But often the most effective way to complete a project or solve a problem is to identify what you want at the end of the project and then figure out how to get from here to there. This strategy helps you identify the specific actions you need to take, and that in turn enables you to set deadlines and quantifiable results. Each of your marketing activities should be tied directly to one or more of your specific goals.

Setting your marketing goals, like establishing strategic goals for your business, requires controlled enthusiasm—you don't want to set your goals so low that you're holding back your business, nor do you want to set goals that are unrealistically high and only serve to discourage you when you fail to meet them.

I encourage new entrepreneurs to set four or five annual goals that reflect the different aspects of their business. Here are some examples:

- My business will net (after expenses) $_____ this year.
- I'll have ____ paying clients within twelve months.
- I'll develop at least __ prospects in this/these industry/ies: _____.
- I'll give at least __ presentation(s) to groups of likely prospects.

- I'll develop ____ new product(s) or service(s) this year based on what I know my clients value.
- I'll take an active volunteer role within the _____ association or group, which will result in ____ clients or referrals within twelve months.

As you're reading this list, I encourage you to sit back—right now—and take a couple of deep breaths. It may feel impossible to guess what your business will look like in a year, so how could you possibly come up with tangible goals now? As I realized when I sat down to write my first marketing plan, the only way I can measure the effectiveness of my marketing is by seeing how close I am to meeting my long-term goals. It wasn't an easy exercise the first time around, and I made several modifications to my goals during the year, based on what I learned about my clients' needs. I still feel a twinge in my stomach as I write down my annual goals because I always set goals that push my comfort zone. I look at this annual exercise as an opportunity to build up my capacity to operate while simultaneously feeling scared or anxious.

> *No one grades you on your marketing plan.*

Fortunately, no one grades you on your marketing plan. You consult your plan in the privacy of your office at least once a week to ensure that you're spending your nonbillable time as effectively as possible. As you'll see in the section below on creating your marketing plan, you'll pause every few months to evaluate what's working, what isn't, and what you need to do next. It's an organic document that evolves as your business grows and you find out which of your assumptions turned out to be off.If you're intimidated by the thought of writing up your goals or if you're tempted to spend time procrastinating rather than writing out your goals, you might want to go back to Chapter 3, *The Mind of an Entrepreneur,* for tips on motivating yourself.

Marketing for Reluctant Entrepreneurs

Many generic marketing-plan templates for small businesses assume that your business will be a storefront operation and that you'll be marketing to local customers. The techniques that work for that market are often not effective for one-person professional businesses because we tend to get our business through referral rather than advertising, and we often don't have a storefront where we could post signs or entice passersby.

One of the most important goals in designing your marketing plan is to *attract* clients rather than chasing after them. With very few exceptions, cold calling and direct mail are not effective ways to bring in clients; your clients are much more likely to go to someone they know personally, through a referral or recommendation, or by reputation. Your marketing plan will include various activities for engaging your prospective clients rather than just talking to them.

The steps you take to raise your profile with your clients depend on your clients and the products or services you offer. Following are three categories of marketing that are usually effective for entrepreneurs. You'll find plenty of specific ideas in Chapter 10, *Brand "You."*

Word-of-Mouth Marketing

Eventually most of your clients will come to you because they heard about you specifically. But that word-of-mouth marketing has to start somewhere, and you have to be that first mouth. Activities to create word-of-mouth referrals include public speaking, publishing an e-newsletter or blog, actively networking, offering workshops and seminars, and so on.

> *Design your marketing strategy to*
> *attract clients rather than chase after them.*

Building this kind of marketing momentum takes time; people will recommend you to others after they've already gotten to know, trust, and value you. This doesn't always mean that you have to meet people one-on-one or take people out for coffee every day. Rather, you'll use the techniques described in Chapter 10, *Brand "You,"* to get in front of prospective clients regularly so that they see you as a reliable, trustworthy professional.

Becoming a Trusted Expert

People like working with people they trust. Your marketing plan will include a variety of activities that enable you to establish a reputation as someone who is an acknowledged expert in her field. This can be difficult for those of us who absorbed the childhood message of not bragging about oneself or, as Australians say, cutting tall poppies down to size.

Thankfully, there are plenty of marketing activities you can use to promote yourself without feeling overly boastful. Having strong content on your blog and website, writing for publications your clients read, taking on a leadership role in a professional group, and offering webinars on research-related topics are all ways you can establish your credibility without feeling that you are overtly tooting your own horn. In fact, the most difficult aspect of becoming seen as an expert is being brave enough to see yourself as a thought leader. (And if you are hyperventilating right now, return to Chapter 3, *The Mind of an Entrepreneur,* for some tools to see yourself as the expert you are.)

Creating News

The final category of marketing activities is creating publicity about yourself. This might include sending out a press release about a survey you conducted, being featured in an article or interviewed on the radio or a webcast, or even having your web site linked to from an influential blog. Becoming media-friendly involves thinking like a reporter—you need to offer something that is truly newsworthy to your potential clients and the reporter's readers, and to package it in a way that makes it easy for the reporter to turn your news into a story. A useful resource for raising your visibility through getting media exposure is Steven Van Yoder's book, *Getting Slightly Famous: Become a Celebrity In Your Field and Attract More Business with Less Effort.*

Writing Your Marketing Plan

While the specific format doesn't matter, it's important that you design a marketing plan that enables you to see your strategic goals for the year as well as the week-to-week activities you've planned. You may have to modify your plan as the year progresses, so it needs to be organized in a way that enables you to make changes as you go along. You can expect to spend at least a couple of hours a day marketing until your business is well established. Expect to have several marketing efforts going on simultaneously. Some of your efforts may be done within a month or two, and some will be ongoing. (Chapter 10, *Brand "You,"* provides examples of various types of marketing strategies.)

As you develop your marketing plan, look at each of your tangible goals for the year and think about what activities will move you toward those goals. Say one of your goals is to get ten new clients in the next year. Your strategies may include actively participating in professional groups your clients attend, writing a newsletter and blog, and presenting a webinar of interest to your clients. You may find that some of these strategies require sequential actions while others simply involve three simultaneous activities. Tailoring a marketing plan to how you work enables you to keep track of your various projects and to track the effectiveness of each one.

Remember, the point of the plan is to help you see how much progress you've made and whether you need to modify any of your approaches. This ensures that you spend your valuable time—the hours you work and aren't getting paid—most effectively so that you can achieve the bigger goals in your life. If you go into your office in the morning and can't figure out what to do to get your business going, look at your marketing plan. If that doesn't give you enough guidance, the plan needs work.

Below are three examples of marketing plan formats for entrepreneurs. Although they're each formatted differently, they share a few important features.

- Your goals for the year are at the top of every page.
- You can clearly see what actions you have planned for each week or month.
- You can see your progress and identify what needs your attention

Timeline

The timeline format lets you see all of your marketing efforts for six months or more on one page. It's clear when an activity is dependent on something else getting done first, which simplifies how you prioritize your time.

Timeline Marketing Plan

Marketing Timeline: {year}							
Goals for the year:							
• Have 5 paying clients by end of year • $30K revenue by end of year • Prof assn activity yielding 5 referrals by end of year							
Activity	Jan	Feb	Mar	Apr	May	Jun	Jul
Social media (contribute, participate)							
ID clients' social media hangouts							
Conduct reality-check interviews							
Monitor, comment on 5 blogs, tweet streams							
Evaluate results: am I moving toward my goals?							
Networking (f2f, virtual)							
ID local groups through MeetUp, prof assns, etc.							
Attend 3 meetings of each group							
Evaluate which groups have *likely* clients							
Attend their meetings regularly, volunteer							
Evaluate results: am I moving toward my goals?							
Volunteer work							
ID (non-virtual) assns or groups of clients							
Evaluate, decide which to participate in							

Many thanks to Kathryn Borden for the format of this marketing plan.

Calendar

The calendar format allows you to schedule time for each of your marketing projects on specific days. If you tend to lose track of time and find that a week goes by and you haven't gotten much done, this could be a useful format for staying focused.

Calendar Marketing Plan

Month				
Goals for the year			**Projects for this month**	
1) Have 5 paying clients by end of year 2) Bring in $30,000 by end of first year 3) Active volunteer in client assn, resulting in 5 referral end of year			1) Contact assn president, line up client-facing volunteer job 2) Guest-blog for assn 3) ID conferences to speak at in 9-12 months 4) Conduct 4 reality-check interviews	
Monday	Tuesday	Wednesday	Thursday	Friday
_1_|	_2_|	_3_|	_4_|	_5_| Do research in assn web site. Where's a good fit for me?
_8_| ID 5 LinkedIn contacts for reality-check interviews	_9_| ID assn leadership; send email, set up time to talk	_10__|	_11__|	_12__| Follow up on LinkedIn contacts. How many more should I contact?
_15__|	_16__|	_17__|	_18__|	_19__|

Free-form

The free-form marketing plan is for people who don't like marketing plans. There's plenty of room to doodle and make notes, and this format allows you to tackle your marketing projects whenever you feel inspired. Put gold stars next to your completed activities. Go wild!

Free-form Marketing Plan

<u>January</u> To-Do List

Goals for the year:
- Have 5 paying clients by end of year
- $30K revenue by end of year
- Active volunteer in client assn, resulting in 5 referrals by end of year

---

ID clients' key social media hangouts

Conduct 5 reality-check interviews, write up what I learned
> ID pain points of prospective clients, develop into speaking topic

ID local groups
> Look through MeetUp, professional assns, Facebook
> Attend 3 meetings of each group, meet people
> Evaluate which group(s) have likely clients

NOTES:

Talked with John B at Acme → recommended I call Robin at High Corp. & JK at Market Corp.

You can download templates for all of these plans at reluctant-entrepreneur.com.

What's Not Working?

Be sure to build checkpoints into your marketing plan so that every two or three months you can evaluate your progress toward your larger goals. Are you as successful as you had expected? If not, your first impulse may be to abandon that effort and try something else. Resist that urge! Often, a marketing initiative that doesn't seem to be effective just needs to be adjusted based on what you have learned so far.

The disconnect between you and the people who need, want, and value what you offer could be caused by a number of factors, any one of which could be sending an unclear or confusing message to your prospective clients. Before you give up on any marketing approach, look at each of the aspects of your plan and ask yourself what you could change to get a better result. Here is where most entrepreneurs run into trouble:

- The audience—WHO you are talking to
  Are you sure that you're talking with potential buyers? It might be time to do a few more reality-check interviews described in Chapter 4, *Who Are Your Clients?*

- The message—WHAT you say
  It's your job to communicate your value in a way that your prospective clients hear you. Are you sure that you're talking in a compelling way about the problem you solve or the need you meet for your clients?

- The method—HOW you say it
  You can communicate with your prospective clients through a wide variety of media and techniques. Are your clients likely to see your Twitter posts or are they more likely to be reading an article in a peer-reviewed academic journal?

- The timing—WHEN you talk with your clients and how consistently your clients hear your message
  Are you at the right part of a budget cycle? Are you catching

them when they care about what you're talking about? And have they heard you enough times that they recognize your name?

Twenty Ways to Kick-Start Your Marketing

Even after years in business, you'll have times when it seems that you barely have the energy to drag yourself into your office, and you can't stand the thought of having to go out and generate business. You suddenly notice that business has dropped off and you can't seem to get back into the swing of marketing. The following are some of the actions you can add to your marketing plan when you need to reinvigorate your marketing.

1. Directly ask for referrals from your existing clients.
   "Who do you know who needs <insert your key value here> whom I might contact?" People need to be reminded to pass your name along to their friends and colleagues.
2. Get in touch with your clients, just to check in.
   I never cease to marvel at how effective a "just calling to say hi" call is to generate additional business from repeat customers.
3. Revisit your existing client list.
   Evaluate who your best clients have been in terms of project budgets, repeat business, and referrals. Think about what these clients have in common and how you found them. Where could you find other clients like these?
4. Look through your social networks.
   If you haven't established connections with all of your clients, now is the time to do it. And see who their contacts are; if you see any who you think may use your services, ask your client for a connection or introduction.

5. Reach out to clients with new offerings.
   If you identify a new issue or concern to your clients' businesses, design a specific product or service that would address your clients' specific needs and send a (hard copy) letter to your clients, telling them about your new offering.

6. Write an article for a publication that your clients read.
   It need not be long, and it should be practical and nontechnical.

7. Write ten blog posts and queue them up for posting over the next couple of months.
   Don't have a blog yet? Now is the time to get one started.

8. Prepare for and conduct three reality-check interviews with prospects in an industry or area that is new to you.
   Learn what its specific pain points are and develop an approach to market to this industry. For more discussion of reality-check interviews, see Chapter 4, Who Are Your Clients?

9. Identify a current topic of interest to your client base.
   Conduct your own survey of your network; this is a great time to ping your clients, colleagues, and prospects. Write up the results into a white paper, promote it on your web site, and notify all your clients of the availability of your resource.

10. Commit to three networking outings a week.
    This could be anyone from a colleague to a prospect to a client. Take a friend to lunch and focus on building your mutual networks. Ask him what kinds of leads he'd like to hear about. Depending on what he does, that might be sales referrals, job opportunities, leads for good employees, or client projects. Tell him what kinds of clients you're specifically looking for.

11. Use an obscure holiday as a reason to send out greeting cards to your clients and prospects.

I still remember a family friend who sent out annual cards for Groundhog's Day, just because it was fun. The spring or fall equinox, the Queen's Birthday, Mardi Gras, or even something as silly as International Respect for Chickens Day (May 4) can serve as a reason for sending a card. And yes, I'm talking about actual note cards, the kind that are made of paper, usually folded in half with a place to handwrite your thoughts, which you then place in an envelope, address, stamp, and place in the mailbox.

12. Check the social network profiles of your clients, and if they list their birthday, send a card.

13. Call a colleague and ask her how her business is doing. Ask her what was the most important change she has made to her business in the last year. Share an interesting resource with her.

14. Call someone who is reliably upbeat and positive. That kind of energy is contagious.

15. Identify one new group that your prospective clients are likely to belong to, join it, and evaluate how you can volunteer strategically in a member-facing capacity.

16. Attend a local meeting of a group you find interesting, even if you don't expect to find clients. Consider the visit to be professional development, not just marketing. I sometimes find my best clients when I'm not looking for them.

17. Schedule a meeting of your advisory board. If you don't have an advisory board, this is a good reason to set one up. Identify four or five people you respect, people who understand the issues of running a professional services business and who are willing to give you honest feedback. Ideally, these people live in your general area and can meet with you. If that's not possible, build a virtual advisory board that meets online.

18. Look at your upcoming trips and identify clients and prospects in those cities.
    Send notes letting them know you'll be in the neighborhood and would like to set up a time to meet. (When I travel, I always arrive early on the day before a speaking engagement so that I have time to meet clients or prospects wherever I go.)
19. Upgrade your professional networks.
    Review all your professional listings in the professional associations you belong to, on your social networks, and anywhere else your company is listed. Upgrade and freshen up your listings, revising them to target your current market and to reflect your clients' current concerns.
20. Throw a party.
    Host a monthly get-together for your clients where they can relax, network, and—incidentally—remember how much they enjoy working with you. Make it a regular event—your clients know that you'll be hosting a happy hour on the first Monday of the month, for example.

Five Marketing Plan Essentials

- View your marketing plan as a work in progress; review it monthly.
- To achieve your strategic goals for the year, plan backward from your end point.
- Set tangible, realistic, measurable goals.
- Plan activities that create word of mouth, build your brand, and create publicity.
- Use your marketing plan to make the best use of your time.

10 Brand "You"

One of the biggest challenges most entrepreneurs face is marketing. Having a clear strategy enables you to spend your marketing time most effectively. This chapter looks at how to talk about yourself and your business in ways that feel comfortable to you and that communicate your value to the people you want as clients.

You're the Expert

An expert is someone who has value, knows her value, can easily demonstrate that value, and isn't afraid to be well compensated for her value. Experts don't offer their services for free; they don't respond to requests to "work for free because this will help your portfolio"; they don't bother responding to mass solicitations in which their likelihood of getting the project is low. Experts find that clients come to them—they don't have to chase after clients.

> *Create the reputation as the best—and only—person who does exactly what you do, in exactly the way you do it. Start acting like the expert you are.*

Does this sound like an easier way to make a living? Would you like to be seen as an expert? Fortunately, you don't have to wait for someone to anoint you; you don't have to go through an application process. Here's the secret: You create the (presumably justified) reputation as the best—and only—person who does exactly what you do, in exactly the way you do it. In other words, you start acting like the expert you are.

Uh-oh. That means you have to *believe* that you offer a unique service that some segment of the population will find wildly valuable. If you're at a loss for what that special something is, go back to your notes from your reality-check interviews, which I discuss in Chapter 4, *Who Are Your Clients?* Remind yourself of what the people you talked with said—what do they really need, what would they really value if it were offered? Then think about why you're an entrepreneur, however reluctant—what is it that you love to do and that you do really well? How are you using your brilliance to help your clients solve a problem or fill a need? Your answers to these questions tell you why you're qualified to call yourself an expert.

When I started my business, I had periodic bouts of the Imposter Syndrome—a fear that I was unprepared to do this work and that everyone would find out that I'm just a fake. (For more about the Imposter Syndrome, see Chapter 3, *The Mind of an Entrepreneur.*) I eventually developed an inner response to my inner critic, which I would practice saying out loud regularly. "I love what I do and I'm really good at it." Eventually I became more comfortable looking someone in the eye and saying that, without bursting out laughing.

> *Look at yourself from your client's perspective*
> *and describe why your clients use you.*

Much of becoming an expert comes down to behaving like one. Share as much as you can, in a blog, on your web site, in a short video, or wherever your clients are. The message you're effectively communicating is that you can afford to "give away" valuable insights because you have so much more to offer your clients.

On my web site, I post the slide decks to my recent presentations, podcasts on topics of interest to my clients, and other resources my clients would find useful. I used to worry that someone might take my slide deck and give a presentation as if it were their own material. Then I realized that what I'm paid for as a speaker isn't an outline on slides—my goals are to convey insight, inspire, and provoke thought, and none of that is captured in a slide deck. By sharing my content, I'm showing that my value isn't just in the information I can convey but the ideas I generate.

The language you use when talking about yourself and your business also conveys a message. You want your listener to know that you offer a customized service that your clients highly value. Instead of describing what you do, learn to talk about what happens with your clients after they've hired you. Look at yourself from your clients' perspective and describe why your clients use you.

Instead of saying you provide counseling services for individuals and families, you could say you help your clients gain insight and live richer lives. Instead of saying you're a CPA who works with small businesses, you could say you help small businesses use their money more strategically. Instead of describing how you transcribe audio recordings, you could talk about enabling clients to capture insights on the fly.

Managing Multiple Messages

As noted in Chapter 9, *Your (Fabulous) Marketing Plan*, you'll always be working on several marketing approaches simultaneously. Some may be done within a month, some will take six months or more, and some will be ongoing activities. A marketing axiom holds that potential buyers have to be exposed to your "brand" at least seven times before they remember you; your goal is to ensure that buyers hear about you frequently and in a variety of contexts.

An effective marketing plan includes as many avenues and media as you can manage at once and that are relevant to your prospective clients. You'll probably include some of the following in your approaches.

- E-newsletters
  E-mail newsletters can be a tremendous marketing tool. They provide the reader with something useful, they show your expertise, and they serve as a regular reminder to your clients of your services. An e-newsletter doesn't need to be long—three or four paragraphs are plenty—but it needs to be interesting and arrive on a regular schedule. You can build your e-mail subscription list by asking everyone you contact if they'd like a sample issue and following up with an invitation to subscribe.
- Blogs, Twitter, Google+
  Blogs and micro-blogging sites like Twitter are easy ways to

share your ideas, an interesting or thought-provoking article, and links to other blog posts. You can even blog a summary of the article you just wrote for your newsletter, and then tweet a link to the blog post or a copy of the e-newsletter. Blogs are an easy way to share your thoughts like the expert you are and to reach a large number of readers. Keep in mind that blatant self-promotion doesn't work in the blogosphere; if all you do is point to press releases about your latest accomplishments, you'll lose readers.

- Social networks like Facebook and LinkedIn
  Social networks like Facebook and LinkedIn give you an opportunity to connect with people rather than just point to web pages. Join groups within these networks that your clients belong to or where others in your field participate. Add your voice to conversations and keep your profile status updated. There are several schools of thought about who to connect with—everyone who approaches you or just people you have met in person. Use your judgment, keeping in mind that the larger your network, the more valuable it is to you as a marketing tool.

- Image-sharing sites like Instagram, Pinterest, and Tumblr
  If you can effectively convey ideas with pictures, photos, and graphics, social sites that are focused on sharing images may be good places to establish your brand. As with other social networks, you can "follow" people whose posts interest you, and you can encourage your clients to follow you.

- Video-sharing sites like YouTube and Vimeo
  You can create a short video by simply setting up your camera, smart phone, or computer's web cam, smiling into the camera, and talking about what you love the most in your work. Letting people in your market see your face and

hear your voice helps connect you with your prospective clients.

- Articles in publications your clients read
  Writing articles may not be your favorite task; many of us think back on writing assignments in school and shudder. Fortunately, writing for your clients is a lot easier than analyzing the concept of destructive pride in Beowulf. From conversations with your clients and prospective markets, you know what their big pain points are, what they're concerned about, and what they really need. Look through your blog and see which posts generated comments; scan Twitter and see what others in your field are talking about; survey your market about a current interest and write up the results. Once you have a topic, identify the publications that your clients read and that accept articles not written by their own staff. (See the latest edition of *Writer's Market* for more information about individual publications' policies and for pointers to publications in your area of interest.) Many trade and professional associations publish magazines or newsletters as well; see if the groups your clients belong to offer the opportunity for you to contribute to their publications.

- Speaking in front of your prospective clients
  Your clients may attend professional conferences or association chapter meetings where there are speakers. Look at the web site for the conference or chapter to check out the topics they feature, the name of the program organizer, and the procedure for submitting a speaking proposal. (For a local group, you may be able to call the organizer and offer to speak at an upcoming meeting.) Often you'll be pitching your presentation for an event six months or a year out; this is a marketing strategy that requires significant lead time. (If you aren't naturally

comfortable speaking in public, consider joining Toastmasters. They offer great opportunities for learning how to talk comfortably in front of others about yourself, your interests, and your business.)

- Networking events
  Even introverts need to get out of the house every once in a while, and we all benefit from chatting with others in our field. One of your best sources of business is referrals, but people can't refer their friends and colleagues to you until they know you. Find local events through MeetUp.com, and look for local chapters of the organizations your clients and colleagues have joined. While it's fine to hand out your own business cards, it is more important to collect the cards of the people you talk with so that you can follow up afterward with a note. See "The Art of Schmoozing" section below for more information.
- Volunteer activity in associations or groups your clients belong to
  You can talk about the value you provide to your clients, but people are more likely to remember your message when you demonstrate that value. Once you've identified the groups and associations your clients belong to, contact the head of each organization. Introduce yourself, tell the leader what your most strategic strengths are, and ask where you could be of most service. Focus on activities that keep you in front of the members and that emphasize the skills you want your clients to remember. If you're a graphic artist, offer to design the group's promotional material for an upcoming event. If you're an accountant, offer to write a white paper for the group on best practices in accounting, focused on your clients' concerns.

Note that this list of marketing approaches offers you plenty of opportunities to recycle and reuse your material from one medium to another. A newsletter article can also be a blog post; you can tweet a link to the newsletter; you can use your tweets to stimulate ideas on a presentation you could give; you can even use a recent project as fodder for a newsletter article. My approach is to get at least three uses out of everything I write, and with practice I've found that it's surprisingly easy to repurpose content.

Branding Essentials

Everything you do is part of your image, down to your voice-mail greeting and e-mail signature. Every time your clients see you, hear about you, view your web profile, or look at your work product, they're seeing your brand. Fortunately, what those messages say about you are, for the most part, under your control. Since people are likely to find you through a variety of media, it's important to have a presence wherever your clients (virtually) hang out. Be sure to keep your messages consistent across media as well as relevant to each audience.

Getting Personal(ized)

Having a consistent e-mail address is critical for ensuring that your clients can find you; if you change your e-mail address, you run the risk of losing touch with anyone you have not been in touch with recently. If you have not yet registered your own domain, do it now. (A domain name is a web address, like MyFabulousCompany.com.) You don't even need to have a web site ready to launch in order to get a domain, but you do want to have a personalized e-mail address (me@MyFabulousCompany.com) that you can use for all your business correspondence. While many people use a free e-mail service such as Gmail or Yahoo, I recommend that you get a more permanent address that will remain with you when you want or need to use a different e-mail provider, one that advertises you, not Gmail or Yahoo.

> *Most of your business comes from word of mouth and from your reputation. You must be the one who gets that word-of-mouth marketing started.*

You can register a domain and get a customized e-mail address for less than $50 a year; companies such as Yahoo (smallbusiness.yahoo.com), GoDaddy.com, and BlueHost.com offer this service. Be sure to pay for only what you need. While most domain-hosting companies offer all kinds of services, the only feature you must have is an e-mail address and, if you're ready, a simple web site.

You.com

Once you've learned what your clients really value and how to talk about your value to them, you may want to create your web site. (Aren't sure what your clients value? Read about reality-check interviews in Chapter 4, *Who Are Your Clients?*) It doesn't need to be fancy or flashy; you don't even need more than a few pages to begin with. To project a professional image on your site, start with these basics:

- A brief description of your business
  Keep in mind that this is your one chance to market yourself, so have a pithy phrase you can use as your description. Make it compelling enough that people will want to click through from a search results page to view more information about you. Use phrases that emphasize your value to clients. Depending on your business, you might say "helping physicians build their practices,"

"bringing life to your dreams," or "making your special occasion perfect."

- Your credentials and experience
  In addition to college and professional degrees, list professional groups and associations you're active in, significant awards you've received, and any activities that highlight your expertise. Do not include a résumé or CV; you're a business, not someone looking for a job. If you're just starting your business, include descriptions of your prior jobs, written to focus on the skills you want to highlight—managing projects, developing marketing campaigns, or any information from your prior employment that's relevant to demonstrating your expertise now.

- All your contact options
  Include your mailing address, phone number, and e-mail address, along with links to any other relevant ways to contact you, including your Skype address, Twitter handle, and so on.

- An appropriate photograph
  It might be tempting to post a fun selfie of you on the beach sipping a drink with a little umbrella in it, but you want to maintain a professional image throughout the web. Use a skilled (or better yet, professional) photographer; it really makes a difference in terms of quality, and a good photo helps personalize your web site.

Getting Social

It seems that everyone—from the local chimney sweep to Walmart—is on Facebook, Twitter, and half a dozen other social media sites. While you don't have to maintain profiles on every possible network, your clients should be able to find you wherever they are likely to be. For many professionals, LinkedIn is the go-to network for connecting with colleagues and prospective clients. It offers a number of useful features for finding and staying in touch with people you meet; you can also join discussion groups in LinkedIn that your customers are likely to belong to. Facebook has a more casual friends-and-family feel to it, and you may already have a personal account. I recommend that entrepreneurs keep their Facebook updates focused on their business, rather than exclusively posting pictures of their kids, dogs, or that crazy party last weekend. Twitter is another network that business owners use to keep their customers updated on items of interest. Although you're limited to just 140 characters in each Twitter post, it's an effective way to share your thoughts and pointers to useful resources that you come across.

A number of more visually oriented networks, such as Pinterest, Tumblr, and Scoop.it, are also popular ways of keeping in touch and sharing links to useful or thought-provoking material. If you enjoy communicating through pictures, or if your business involves anything that's visually interesting, such as interior design, graphic arts, or even event planning, these may be effective ways of marketing your services to a broader audience.

Whatever networks you choose to participate in, be mindful of the purpose of your social activities. You're establishing your credibility, letting people get to know you, and demonstrating your accessibility. Be sure that each of your profiles includes:

- Your full name
- Your business e-mail address
- Links to your web site and other social networks
- A photo – either a professional head shot or a more casual photo, depending on the network
- A short description of your business

To "friend" or not to "friend" is a question I often hear. Many social networks encourage you to link to or "follow" other people in the network, and there are several schools of thought on whether to connect with people you don't know well. Some people believe that the value of these networks is in the number of connections you can establish with people—the more the better! Others prefer to link only to people they already know and would personally recommend—they see these connections as a form of endorsement and are selective in who they endorse. I take a middle path: I value the depth and breadth of my professional networks, and I'm somewhat selective in making connections. I decline requests from people who don't provide their full name and location or whose profiles look dodgy; I don't need to build my network with people whose photos are R-rated, thank you.

On a related note, think twice about posting links on overly partisan or controversial issues. While you may care passionately about a political candidate or cause, remember that your clients may strongly disagree with your opinions. Create a separate blog or web site where you can espouse whatever you think the world needs to know, and keep your business profiles focused on what you have in common with your clients and community.

Going Hard Copy

As much as we have all gone digital, there is still a need for something as quaint as business cards—not to mention stationery, envelopes, note cards, and all the other accouterments of the hard-copy world. We do still meet people face to face, and—old-fashioned as I am—I believe that sending a thank-you note or follow-up letter on paper makes a positive impact. And while I sometimes see people exchange virtual business cards via wireless devices, in many circumstances the need for something tangible to hand someone else often remains, even if it's just to note the person's Twitter handle or Facebook page.

You can design and order high-quality business cards, note cards, and other stationery at modest prices from office supply companies as well as from web sites like Vistaprint.com and Overnightprints.com. You can upload your own design or use one of their many professional themes; costs run as low as $20 or $30 for several hundred business cards. (Vistaprint also offers free business cards, but their logo appears on the back of the card; I advise that you spend the money and advertise yourself, not someone else.) Be sure that you leave enough blank space on your card so that you can write a note to remind the other person where they met you or what you do. The cost for customized cards is so low that I create specialized cards for every occasion. I even created a special card with a link to an organ donation web site for a client who wanted to raise awareness of the need for organ donations.

Your business card tells others something about you, so consider all of the following aspects as you choose your design and decide what information to include.

- Paper stock
  Make sure it is uncoated heavy card stock that you can write a note on.
- Font and color
  The font should be easy to read, even for the aging eyes of Baby Boomers, and consistent with your business image. Use a white or light background and a black or very dark color for the lettering. If your card isn't easy for your contacts to read, what does that say about how you relate to your clients?
- Contact information
  Include a mailing address as well as your phone number, e-mail address, website URL, and any other necessary contact

points; for some, that might include a pager number, Twitter handle, and so on.

- Bilingual information
  If your client base spans more than one language, consider having your contact information in different languages on each side of the card.

Talking About Yourself

In addition to the various ways you're marketing yourself in print and online, keep in mind that face-to-face conversations are a powerful way for people to get to know you and your business. It's not enough to just put out your shingle; you need to identify what sets you apart, what makes you essential to your prospective clients.

Get in the habit of telling everyone you know about your business. Call or send notes to your family, your friends and social network, colleagues from your last job, your doctor, lawyer, accountant, and anyone else with whom you have a connection. It doesn't have to be a sales pitch. Just tell them, "Here's what I'm doing these days. If I can be of service to you, I'd love to talk. If you know of someone who could use my services, I'd love for you to put us in touch." There is no need to apologize for contacting them or to be modest or self-effacing about your expertise; learning how to feel comfortable telling people about what you do is simply part of being in business.

You may be surprised to find out that people don't always understand the full range of value you can offer to your marketplace. It's easy for your prospective clients to put you in a niche, so take advantage of that to highlight what is most memorable and relevant to them. The cover for this book was designed by Eric Boelts (www.brainbolts.com). I recommend him to people who need a beautiful book jacket, even though this is just a very small part of what Eric does and who he is.

While I may never need the full range of Eric's services, I enthusiastically refer people to him and I expand his reach even further. As you talk about yourself to prospective clients, be sure you give the other person a way to remember you the way you want to be known. Even if that person doesn't have a need for what you do, he may know other people who do.

Eventually, you'll find that most of your business comes from word of mouth and from your reputation. In the beginning, however, you must be the one who gets that word-of-mouth marketing started. The following are tips for getting people to talk about you and your business.

- Develop a memorable and descriptive ten- or fifteen-second introduction. (See the section below, "So, What Does Your Company Do?" for more on this.)
- Focus on benefits and results, not features; talk about what happens after your clients have worked with you, not just what you do.
- Keep track of how new clients hear about you, and adjust your marketing accordingly.
- Become active in any professional associations you join. Membership alone is not enough. Contribute your skills in an area that's particularly valuable to the group.
- Remind your clients that you appreciate their referral of colleagues to you.
- Find local groups that interest you and where your clients may be.
- Develop a handout or brochure you can offer people –"Six Questions To Ask A Fitness Trainer" or "Ten Tips For New Adoptive Parents."

The Art of Schmoozing

Small talk doesn't come easily for us introverts, and the thought of chatting with perfect strangers fills our hearts with dread. But even those of us who use the grocery store self-check line in order to avoid unneeded conversation with a cashier can learn to become more comfortable talking about our business and ourselves.

A book that I've found tremendously useful in this regard is Debra Fine's, *The Fine Art of Small Talk: How to Start a Conversation, Keep It Going, Build Networking Skills—and Leave a Positive Impression*. Fine is a naturally shy engineer who taught herself how to become a comfortable conversationalist. She shares her tips in this book. She followed that book with another, *The Fine Art of the Big Talk: How to Win Clients, Deliver Great Presentations, and Solve Conflicts at Work*, which takes you from the one-on-one conversations to speaking in settings where there's more at stake.

Whether you're promoting your services at an exhibit booth, attending a local professional association meeting, or just chatting with someone at a meeting, learn about the other person before you start describing your own business. Ask problem-seeking questions to identify ways you can best meet the person's needs. If you're a professional organizer, ask how they stay focused during the day in spite of Facebook, e-mails, phone calls, and the web. If you offer math tutoring, ask how their kids are doing in school and what their biggest challenges are.

As difficult as it is for me to strike up a conversation with a stranger, I had one of those "aha moments" when I realized that most other people are equally shy and are delighted when they find someone willing to listen to what they have to say. The following are reminders that can help you when you're faced with a roomful of people you don't know.

- Be enthusiastic.
  Use your face and body to show emotion and to indicate that you're interested in the conversation. Show that you're

passionate about what you do and that you love working for your clients. (And if that isn't the case, think about refocusing your business on a client base and the type of work that you do love.)

- Be courteous.
  Obviously, you don't arrive late, leave in the middle of a presentation, or engage in antagonistic conversations. Listen at least twice as much as you talk.
- Make yourself memorable.
  Know how to tell a story about your business in a way that makes it easy for listeners to describe your business to others. Think of three words or phrases that connote your value and that you want other people to remember when they think of you.
- Perception is reality.
  Act self-confident even if you don't feel that way, and eventually you'll start feeling as self-assured as you act. Have a firm handshake, smile, and make eye contact with the people you meet.

"So, What Does Your Company Do?"

When someone asks you what you do, do you freeze up or start stammering? You need a concise, memorable response prepared for all the times when you're asked about your work. This is sometimes called your "elevator speech." Why? Imagine stepping into an elevator with your biggest prospect. She turns to you and asks, "So, what exactly do you do?" You have fifteen seconds—the time it takes for the elevator to let her off at the twenty-fifth floor—to describe yourself in such a way that she immediately understands why you're exactly who she needs right now.

Give your elevator speech some careful thought, keeping in mind that everyone you talk to is a potential client or referral source. Paul and Sarah Edwards, the authors of a number of books about home-based businesses, describe a useful formula for developing your fifteen-second introduction. The template they use is this:

"You know how [describe typical clients' problem]? Well, I [solve problem] by [doing this]."

For example, "You know how frustrating it is when you have to make a strategic decision without all the information you need? Well, my company helps you make better decisions by providing you with insight on your competitors." Or, "You know how hard it is to care for elderly parents when you don't live nearby? Well, I coordinate local care for my clients' loved ones throughout the Puget Sound area, and consider each one to be part of my family."

I like this formula because it helps focus on the benefits you provide to your clients, rather than simply describing what you do, and it keeps the entire description to ten or fifteen seconds. Keep the following in mind as you work on your personalized version of the answer to, "So, what do you do?"

- Avoid industry jargon or buzzwords such as "solutions." Word of mouth travels a lot farther if people outside your field understand and can describe to others what you do.
- Keep it short. They're asking you for a reason to use your services, not to hear your life story.
- Make yourself recession-proof. What are your clients' critical needs—things they view as essential, not just nice to have?
- Focus on benefits that provide clear added value. Offer services that your clients can't or won't do for themselves and that enhance their bottom line or the quality of their life.

- Make sure you can deliver your introduction with enthusiasm. If you're excited about your business, others will be as well.

Practice your fifteen-second introduction with everyone you encounter and watch their responses. If you get a blank stare, well, you just learned one way *not* to describe yourself. Keep at it until you've found a few intros that feel genuine, you can say with passion, and that the other person understands. Everyone can be part of your word-of-mouth network if you learn how to effectively convey why people love your product or services so much.

Five Branding To-Do Items

- Register a domain name (URL) for your business, even if you don't need to set up a web site right away.
- Set up accounts on LinkedIn, Facebook, Twitter, and any other social networks where your clients hang out.
- Develop a schedule for sharing your insights and perspective through your online avenues.
- Practice your fifteen-second introduction until you see listeners' eyes light up when you talk about your business.
- Remind everyone you know that referrals are your best source of business.

11 The Reluctantly Strategic Entrepreneur

"No wise fish would go anywhere without a porpoise."
LEWIS CARROLL, FROM *ALICE'S ADVENTURES IN WONDERLAND*

"Strategic planning" sounds so formal—and formidable. Companies dedicate entire departments to this function. But entrepreneurs can, and should, do their own strategic planning as well. It need not involve a Harvard M.B.A.; fortunately, all that is required is the ability to look at your business from an arm's-length perspective once a year and evaluate where you are and where you would like to be heading.

I am not convinced that entrepreneurs need to—or even could—write a strategic business plan extending five years out. In virtually all professional service businesses, there are simply too many variables to predict what the competitive environment will look like or what the business will be doing.

Garth Stein's novel, *The Art of Racing in the Rain,* offers some good insights for anyone dealing with uncertainty. In addition to viewing the world from a dog's perspective—a virtue in itself—this book reminds me that I need to focus more on my end goal and less on the details of how I will get there. As Enzo the dog explains, "The driver who cannot tear his eyes away from the wall as he spins out of control will meet that wall; the driver who looks down the track as he feels his tires break free will regain control of his vehicle."

In that spirit, this chapter looks at when to turn to a new direction, what questions to ask yourself, how to shift your perspective to a more expansive view of what you do for your clients, and what to do next. You'll have to repeat this process yearly because I can predict that you'll encounter some unexpected turns in the road.

Warning: Sharp Curves Ahead

Recently I interviewed a number of long-time entrepreneurs to learn how they recognized that their business needed to change and how they made significant changes in their business. Some had expanded their business, a couple had closed their business, others moved in completely new directions. When I asked them what prompted their change of direction, the same answers kept coming up. As you read this list, consider if any of these issues apply to you and your business.

- "In my field, we constantly have to adapt. The industry changes rapidly, and if you don't keep up, you're left in the dust."
- "I wanted to expand my business, which meant that I had to bring in others. Hiring an assistant gave me the energy and focus to go get new business."
- "I needed to diversify my revenue stream; I realized that I am too dependent on providing a single service to a niche market."
- "The market changed and I found myself competing with 'bottom-feeders'—companies or individuals who were charging a quarter of what I charged—and my clients didn't value my high-end services."

- "I found myself in a rut. I was doing the same old, same old, and I wasn't feeling challenged or energized. I was stagnating, so I needed to stir things up."
- "I was given the chance to work closely with one of my clients." (One of the people I interviewed used this as an opportunity to close her business and work full-time for her client. The other person chose to expand her business with subcontractors so that she could provide more extensive services to her client.)

What I found particularly interesting about these reasons for making a big change was that most of the entrepreneurs felt that they simply had no choice—they *had* to adapt to a changing environment or they would be out of business. While that may sound negative and reactive rather than proactive, in fact it demonstrates a well-functioning early-warning system. Many small businesses are loathe to recognize that their market has changed and that they must change as well. As I was writing this chapter, I read a *Wall Street Journal* article about the problems of near-empty shopping malls. The journalist interviewed a woman who operated a business out of a kiosk in the mall. She said, "I've made my business here. I don't want to move to another mall. I want [this] mall to be like it was eight years ago." While I can sympathize with her longing for the shopping mall to return to its former vitality, choosing not to move to a more economically viable location means that she will likely suffer the same fate as the rest of the mall. If she's willing to change, she might find that she can serve an even better set of customers in a busier mall.

Questions to Ponder

Although we may be reluctant to admit it, many of us make changes only when we have to because we are unsatisfied—for whatever reason—with the status quo. To speed up your planning process and to prompt new ideas, look for things that you're dissatisfied with or situations that you think you could improve. Here are some of the questions I ask myself every year, to help me identify what needs to change.

> *Just as I recognize an issue by the condition of my stomach, so I recognize an inspiration by how much lighter I immediately feel.*

- **What business(es) am I really in?**
  Is there an additional service I could provide that dovetails with my existing services? What business have I wanted to get into this last year?
- **Where is most of my revenue coming from?**
  Is that where I want to be making most of my money? Is there something I do that I could turn into a product? Or would that just turn me into a commodity in the eyes of my clients?
- **What am I really excited about?**
  What do I look forward to working on? What kind of project is particularly satisfying for me? If what I really love to do won't support me directly, how can I take that passion and convert it to a revenue-producing effort?
- **What are the primary markets that I'm known in right now?**
  How strong are those markets? Should I expand to a new field? Do I have the time and energy to face the learning curve of unfamiliar jargon, new issues, and all new players?

I find that the best indicator of an area that I need to focus on is the one that causes my stomach to clench up and try to hide behind my spine. In some years, that might be the question about what really gets me passionate. One year, during my annual strategizing, I recognized that I just wasn't as excited about my work as I used to be and—sure enough—my stomach started tying itself into knots. When I thought back on what had given me the most satisfaction over the past year, I realized that I really enjoyed mentoring other entrepreneurs, and that I was skilled at it. That was when I developed my coaching service, and it continues to be the most rewarding part of my business.

When I had that moment of realization about offering coaching services, I felt like a huge weight had been lifted off my shoulders. When you think you can float on air, you may have just found your new calling.

Planning to Plan
Doing a yearly financial checkup on your business is simple if you've set up your accounting system in a way that lets you easily extract useful information. With most financial management software or services such as QuickBooks, you can set up separate accounts for the different types of work you do. For example, I maintain subaccounts for research, consulting, business coaching, speaking fees, and writing income. Using these separate categories takes no additional effort during the year—I just select the appropriate account when I'm writing each invoice—and doing so makes it easy for me to review my income at the end of the year. I can look at the totals and see exactly how much of my revenue comes from each type of work. In addition, I can categorize my clients by industry or market so that I can monitor where my income is coming from. Think about how you want to monitor your business, and then build the tools that will enable you to do that. And remember, you can always set up new account types and update the account codes in existing invoices as your business grows and diversifies.

Getting a Yearly Checkup

Think of this as your annual visit to the doctor, except without the embarrassing gown that doesn't close in the back. Every year, make an appointment with yourself to sit down and evaluate how your business is doing and, just as important, where you want it to be a year from now. It's easy to coast along from year to year, particularly because we entrepreneurs don't have annual reviews with a boss or annual meetings with a board of directors (isn't that part of the point of being independent?). But if we don't take time to reflect on our business and our competitive environment, we might find ourselves adrift or headed in an unwanted direction.

Set aside a day free of appointments, meetings, or projects. Turn off your phone, clear off your desk, and get ready to think expansively. First, go through your accounts and create a report of your sales for the year, sorted by client. (See the side bar, *Planning to Plan* for thoughts on making this a simpler process. Software such as QuickBooks or an online accounting service such as FreshBooks or QuickBooks Online can produce reports by client and account.) Look at your records on every client for whom you did more than one or two projects. Where did the client come from—a referral from a colleague or another client, a conference you attended, an article you wrote, your blog, a contact from your last job? Ask yourself if you can get more clients from the same source.

What More Can I Do for My Clients?

Look at the kind of work each client has brought you. What else could you do for him? What is driving him these days? Is his business growing or shrinking? What about the industry he's in—is it healthy or struggling? What could you provide to your client to help him expand his business? The late John Levis, a fellow entrepreneur and friend, once told me, "If you're going to grow your business, you need to be able to solve problems. I wound up getting into my field by listening to my clients and understanding their needs, sometimes even when they didn't know what they needed. Most clients are interested in getting answers to solve yesterday's problems; my strategic planning service focuses on solving tomorrow's problems. That's what keeps your clients—and you—in business."

Review your sales records to see if any one of your clients accounts for more than 20 or 25 percent of your revenue. If you find one that fits this criterion, ask yourself:

- What would happen if I lose this client? What impact would that have on my business?
- Why is this client giving me this much work? What can I do to generate similar amounts of revenue from other clients?
- What can I do to provide higher-level, more strategic services to this client? How can I challenge my contacts to make even better use of my expertise and insight?

The practice of reviewing how much revenue each client brings in also helps you recognize how much business a "small" client may give you, cumulatively, over the course of a year. I remember my shock upon realizing the number of projects one consultant had sent me over a period of six months. It was all in one- or two-hour increments so I never thought of her as a particularly large client, but the business she sent my way certainly added up.

After I've reviewed the work I've done for my clients over the past year, I generate a report of income sources—how much I made from research, how much from consulting work, how much from speaking fees, and so on. I try to keep my income stream diversified. Even if one industry, geographic region, or group of clients is hit hard by an economic downturn, other clients may be unaffected. This means that my revenue isn't affected as severely as it would be if all my work came from one small market niche in my local area. Having different types of clients and offering a variety of services also helps even out the workflow over the course of the year; a slow period for one group of clients may be a busy time for another.

Not only do I review the diversity of my revenue sources, I also consider whether and how I might like to change that mix in the coming year. Do I want to travel more or less? Are my webinars profitable? If so, how can I increase the number that I do in a year? What impact will that have on my ability to maintain the other parts of my business?

I also think about maintaining a mix of clients and markets that respond quickly to marketing efforts—perhaps small clients with quick-turnaround projects who need to be reminded to call me—and big-ticket spenders who require more, longer-term marketing approaches. With a blend of both types of clients, I can continually market to the latter group and can ratchet up my marketing efforts to the former group if I find that I'm not as busy as I would like to be and I want to bring in some revenue quickly.

Saying "Thank You"

I do the annual review of my business in December, when the pace of my business is a little slower. As I look at the work I've done for my steady clients, I want to express my gratitude for their business over the year. That brings up the question of whether or how to send holiday gifts to clients. Some entrepreneurs send boxes of candy, fruit, or snacks to their good clients. Others make a donation in their client's name to a noncontroversial charity. But some people worry either that clients will expect generous gifts every year, or that corporate policy prohibits them from accepting gifts from vendors.

I don't have a set policy on gift giving; it depends on my relationship with the client. For a couple of clients I know well,

I donate to a charity I know they support. For a speechwriter client, I sometimes send a book I think he would enjoy. One of my favorite clients gets flowers every so often, just because I know she likes them, and I want to tell her that I'm thinking of her.

Having been on the receiving end of vendors' holiday gifts, I know that the thought really does count. I don't keep track of who sent me something last year and who didn't, but I do remember the occasional gift that shows that someone really thought of me. I forget within a month who sent me a tin of popcorn but I remember for years a gift that has special value or personal meaning. One year, a publisher I worked for sent me a beautiful print of a photo he had taken in the Sierra Nevada Mountains. I'll always be grateful for that one gift, and I hope that one day I'll be able to give a client something with equal impact.

Am I Root-bound or a Bonsai?

One of the problems you may experience when you've been in business for a while is consistently having more work coming in than you can comfortably fit into a day. If you find yourself at that point, you may feel as constricted as did the root ball of the long-suffering Norfolk pine that lives in the corner of my living room. It was looking forlorn, and a glance at its base told me that it had outgrown its pot and needed more room to support its nine feet of trunk. In order for it to grow, I knew I needed to commit to the work and mess of repotting it; otherwise, the prognosis for its continued health was not good.

On the other hand, a friend of mine cultivates bonsai plants. The patience and care she gives them is extraordinary, and she's repaid by having a perfectly formed juniper, seemingly bent over from years in the wind, but in miniature. For her, growth for the sake of growth has no appeal; she's more interested in creating something on a scale that she enjoys, and that requires as much focus as someone maintaining a forest of plants in their living room. Either approach can work well, and—as in horticulture—you have many options between the extremes of a bonsai maple and a maple tree towering fifty feet overhead.

> *Build relationships with your clients; they need to have confidence in you before they entrust you with a large project.*

This may be a good time for you to sit back and evaluate in which direction you want your business to go. What are your long-term goals and aspirations for your professional life? One of the following may resonate with you:

- You want to build a business that you can eventually sell. In this case, your focus should be to create a strong company brand, hire employees who are committed to your clients, and ensure that your clients are loyal to your company, not just to you personally. As your business can support it, continue to hire full-time employees to do as much of the work as possible so that you can present a stand-alone business to prospective buyers.
- You want to make a high salary so that you can support yourself through your retirement. You may need a reliable group of contractors or employees who can handle a percentage of your work; alternatively, you can focus on providing higher and higher value so that you can continually raise your prices to reflect your increasing value. Your goal is to develop services that allow you to double your income without doubling your workload; if your income is tied to the number of hours you work, you won't be able to expand beyond the number of hours you can work in a day.

- You want to build a successful business, but your goal is not to make a high salary.

  Let's say you have a bonsai business. You market aggressively when you need to, but you're more interested in cultivating the clients you have than in bringing in new clients. You may find that you're consciously or subconsciously making choices that limit your growth. As long as you recognize these choices and think through the consequences, opting to turn down projects that require you to expand your business may be an appropriate way to keep your business at the size you want it.

If you start feeling root-bound by having more work than you have the time or resources to handle, it may be time to consider enlarging your pot. You could do this by bringing in a business partner, hiring employees—either full- or part-time— or using contractors as the need arises. Each of these choices has its own challenges, but the contracting option is usually the least risky and one that you can either expand or pull out of if necessary.

With Clients, Is More Always Better?
My approach has been to look for steady clients; that is, clients I can rely on for repeat business and who engage me for big-budget projects. Generally, these kinds of clients are less price sensitive, they understand the added value I can provide, they're more likely to use me consistently, and my contacts often refer me to colleagues or other departments I can serve. When I have a mix of steady clients, I feel financially stable; I have (reasonably) reliable revenue from a variety of sources, so my cash flow will be steady and I can cut back on my short-term marketing efforts.

Be careful, though, of becoming too dependent on any one client. Things happen in organizations, often with little warning. Your main contact may leave the company. The organization may have a spending freeze or merge with another organization. Your client's priorities shift and she decides to move in a direction that doesn't include you. If you count on any one client for more than 25 percent of your income, you're putting your business at risk when—not if— you lose that client and have to immediately find new clients to replace the lost revenue.

Smaller clients—in terms of budget or number of projects— can also be great clients, as long as they use you regularly and are good referral sources. On the other hand, keep in mind that it often takes as much work to get a small client as it does a big one, and you want to make sure that you see a good "return" on the time you spend marketing.

I think of building my client base as I would build a stone wall: The base should be composed of large, stable rocks, but I need the smaller rocks and mortar to support and hold together the larger boulders. As long as I have a healthy mix of clients, I know my business—or my wall—will last.

Moving to the Next Level

If you want to build your business rather than keep it as a bonsai company, you'll always be watching for opportunities to expand your income stream by increasing the projects or client engagements that are more profitable than the average client. There are a number of ways to cultivate these larger projects, both by expanding your existing clients' understanding of the range of your services and by reaching out to new groups of clients. Note that these are not mutually exclusive—you can expand your engagement with your existing clients at the same time that you move into other markets or groups of clients.

Expanding Through Natural Growth

One of the easiest ways to get larger projects from your clients is simply to ask. Clients may not know the extent of your services, so they would not necessarily think of you for projects or engagements that are more complex than usual. I try to work in a casual reference to a recent large job when I'm chatting with a client; this way, she's reminded that, yes, I handle large projects.

Build relationships with your clients. They need to have confidence in you before they entrust you with a large project with high stakes. That may mean working with them on a volunteer project for a professional association you both belong to, or getting together with your client every few months for lunch or coffee—assuming you're in the same city.

I hadn't realized how much impact those personal connections have until Boulder, Colorado, (where I live) suffered massive flooding in 2013. I was touched by the clients who reached out to see how I was doing and to inquire if there was anything they could do to help. (Fortunately, my home came through unscathed.) A couple of clients even sent a donation to the local flood relief fund—those are clients I will now walk through walls for.

Move toward a more consultative role with your clients. There's a fine art to the initial conversation you have with a client about a project. As you conduct the initial assessment of what your client needs, watch for opportunities to provide extra value that your client might not have thought to ask for. Think about what else you could do that does not require much more from you and that serves to delight your client, keeping in mind that the approach you take depends on your business and your clients. For example, the home inspector I used when I bought my last house gave me a great home-maintenance book in addition to his report. A landscape designer I knew offered a free annual "tune-up" of all the gardens he designs. Even my dog groomer offers a massage (for my dog, that is) at the end of her appointment. All of these are ways that business owners can demonstrate that they care about their clients and want to make their services even more valuable to them.

Building a New Client Base

While it's often easier to expand work from existing clients than it is to find new clients, the latter is sometimes the best approach. If your current client base tends to be overly budget conscious or isn't able to pay you according to your value, it may be time to move to a market that offers more profitable clients.

Remember when you identified your client base when you started your business? See Chapter 4, *Who Are Your Clients?*, to remind you of how to focus on the best prospective clients and how to tailor your services to meet the critical needs of your market. Your criteria will probably have changed significantly from when you started your business. You now know what kinds of services are the most rewarding and profitable for you and what kinds of clients you want to attract.

Just as it took time to build your initial group of clients, it takes time to build a new client base. Expect this to extend over the course of a year or more before you truly benefit from your efforts, keeping in mind that the investment of your time will pay off in more profitable clients down the road. Identify industry conferences that are nine months to a year out, and decide whether it would be beneficial for you to attend, exhibit, or speak at the conference, and take the appropriate actions. If you aren't yet a member of the association your prospective clients belong to, join and start volunteering in a member-facing role. Employ all the other techniques you used when you built your initial client base, focusing now on your new market.

Remember that it takes time to establish a professional reputation; start getting in front of your new prospects early and often, and treat this with as much energy and focus as you had when you began your business.

Building a Brain Trust

While Franklin Roosevelt was governor of New York and during his first term as president, he had an informal group of advisors whom he consulted regularly; he referred to that group as his Brain Trust. Consider taking a cue from F.D.R.; a small cadre of advisors can be immensely helpful. As one- or two-person businesses, we sometimes lose that broader perspective, and we all can benefit from ideas and feedback from people outside our business.

Some entrepreneurs create relatively formal advisory boards, consisting of selected clients, colleagues, and others who understand the issues pertaining to their type of business. Others simply pull together small groups of clients for dinner and brainstorming. And some people have a few individuals they talk with regularly who are reliable sounding boards. What matters is that you identify people who understand your business, who are articulate, whose instincts you trust, and who are committed to your success.

Engage the members of your brain trust regularly, either in face-to-face meetings or individual conversations. Ask hard questions—"Am I still on top of my game or do I need to develop in some area?" "Is my value message clear or should I refocus?" "What three changes would you recommend for my business?" And, harder yet, be open to their answers, remembering that you need not implement every suggestion you hear.

If you're not comfortable asking clients or colleagues to offer their thoughts, consider contacting SCORE (formerly known as the Service Corps of Retired Executives), which is sponsored by the U.S. Small Business Administration (www.score.org). A volunteer from SCORE can help you think through where your business is going and how you want to get there. SCORE offers both face-to-face and e-mail counseling at no charge, as well as webinars, business tools, and online workshops, all in support of small businesses.

> *What do you want so much that you will push yourself past your comfort zone to achieve it?*

Some entrepreneurs prefer to work with a business consultant or coach; if your finances are tight, see if the coach will agree to a barter of your services in exchange for help with strategic planning. One of my clients noted that a key benefit of hiring a coach was that she was demonstrating her faith in her business by investing money in building her entrepreneurial skills.

Making the Shift

OK, you know what steps you need to take in order to move your business forward. Here comes the easy part—just doing it—right? Simple perhaps, but not necessarily easy. I've developed a five-step process for creating a strategic plan I can actually use.

1. List the goals and dreams you have for your business. What do you want your business to look like in a year? Your goals may include getting five new clients, creating a group of advisors for your business, earning a certain amount of money, learning a new skill, or expanding into a new field.
2. Identify the first few approaches or strategies you need to take toward those goals.

They may be modified after you have a chance to see how effective your approaches are, and you may not even know what all is involved in each strategy. Your approaches may include becoming active in an association or professional group, writing an e-book your clients would value, developing a blog, or becoming active in social networks.

3. For each of these approaches, identify the first few tangible tasks or action steps you need to accomplish.
   Make them clear enough that you know when you've completed each step. A task could be researching and evaluating blog hosts, recording a podcast, printing business cards, or developing a survey of your prospective clients.

4. Complete at least one task for each of your big goals each week.
   If a task will take more than a week to complete, make sure you're continuing to make quantifiable progress on each of your goals. Even if you're busy with current work, it's crucial to set aside time to invest in ensuring that your business will grow in the direction you want.

5. As you complete each task, go back to Step 3, look at each of your approaches, and decide what the next few action steps are.

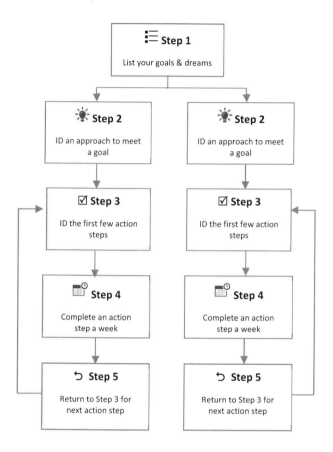

It isn't glamorous, but I find this structure to be useful for moving me in a new direction. If you're familiar with David Allen, known for his *Getting Things Done* book and program, you'll recognize the GTD process of breaking big goals down into their component parts and then identifying two or three tangible action items to be accomplished for each component.

I've talked with hundreds of entrepreneurs about their businesses, particularly about how they overcome obstacles to their success. One thing I hear consistently is, "Failure is not an option." Some people are paying a child's college tuition, some are the primary earner in the household, and some simply cannot imagine going back to a traditional job. One of the biggest rewards for me is the ability to create whatever kind of business I want, doing what I love to do. What do *you* want so much that you'll push yourself past your comfort zone to achieve it?

When I need to make a strategic shift in my business, one thing that keeps me focused and moving forward is thinking of how great it is going to be *after* I've accomplished my goal. I know that I'll be re-energized with this challenge, and I keep reminding myself of that when I have trouble getting motivated. Trust me—it's how this book got written!

Five Tips for Making Strategic Change

- Consider all your options; don't make a decision based on fear, indecision, or a belief that you have no choice.
- You have to be willing to fail in order to take reasonable risks. If you never fail, you aren't trying hard enough.
- If an idea doesn't work out, remind yourself that you didn't fail—the idea just didn't work out.
- Make your own decisions; don't be overly influenced by what did or didn't work for others.
- Follow your passion. If you have an idea that gets you energized and makes you feel ten years younger, go with it!

Appendix A: Resources for Entrepreneurs

Duct Tape Marketing
ducttapemarketing.com
> John Jantsch, public relations guru for entrepreneurs and author of *Duct Tape Marketing*, offers a number of free e-books and other resources on his web site. He focuses on using social media and building relationships with clients.

Freelancers Union
freelancersunion.org
> This nonprofit has a very broad focus; in addition to a wide range of resources and an active blog, Freelancers Union offers health, liability, and disability insurance. As you might think from its name, this organization is focused on the interests and concerns of one-person businesses, and even hosts "un-office parties" for members.

Gateway to Associations
asaecenter.org
> The American Society of Association Executives maintains a directory of trade and professional associations, useful for entrepreneurs who want to identify groups whose members are prospective clients. From the main ASAE web page, type "gateway to associations" in the search box, or go directly to the web site:

www.asaecenter.org/Community/Directories/AssociationSearch.cfm

Getting Things Done
gettingthingsdone.com
>David Allen, author of *Getting Things Done*, has created a wide range of resources to help people get organized and stay productive, including downloads of webinars and podcasts, discussion forums, and guides for getting your GTD system set up and running smoothly.

Seth Godin
sethgodin.com
>Seth Godin is a marketing consultant and author who understands how businesses can connect with their clients by being authentic. His web site is full of resources, ideas, and tips for effectively communicating with customers.

Healthcare.gov
>One of the biggest impediments many would-be entrepreneurs cite to starting a business is a concern that they won't be able to afford health insurance. Obamacare has made it easier for the self-employed to get affordable health insurance directly from the carriers. Start at healthcare.gov to find what plans are available in your state.

Kauffman Foundation
entrepreneurship.org
>The Ewing Marion Kauffman Foundation established Entrepreneurship.org to serve as a resource for entrepreneurs who have great ideas. This web site includes hundreds of articles, audio and video recordings, and other tools addressing a wide range of issues relevant to entrepreneurs.

Office Space
>This 1999 movie features disgruntled software engineers dealing with a passive-aggressive boss and two consultants named Bob who are downsizing the office. The protagonist

tells a hypnotist, "So I was sitting in my cubicle today, and I realized, ever since I started working, every single day of my life has been worse than the day before it. So that means that every single day that you see me, that's on the worst day of my life." This movie always serves as an antidote to the "lure" of working for a boss.

Practice Trumps Theory

practicetrumpstheory.com

Ash Maurya blogs about a wide variety of topics of interest to entrepreneurs, ranging from how to interview clients to creating metrics that help you to make better decisions. While many of his examples feature products rather than professional services, much of the advice applies to both.

Reluctant Entrepreneur

reluctant-entrepreneur.com

My blog includes updated thoughts related to being a reluctant entrepreneur, as well as templates and other resources to supplement this book.

SCORE

score.org

SCORE (formerly the Service Corps of Retired Executives) provides free mentoring as well as a wide range of free and low-cost resources for entrepreneurs, including webinars, workshops, articles, templates, and business tools. Check out the SCORE chapter in your area for information on local events.

Toastmasters

toastmasters.org

Every entrepreneur needs to be able to communicate effectively and speak confidently. Gack! If the thought of making a presentation fills you with dread, join a local Toastmasters group. You will have weekly opportunities to practice your speaking skills in a supportive environment. Many excellent speakers credit Toastmasters for their success.

U.S. Small Business Administration
sba.gov

> The SBA has a great collection of resources for entrepreneurs. While some of its material is more directed to retail and storefront businesses, plenty of the material is useful for any entrepreneur. The SBA also supports Small Business Development Centers in every state, which provide free and low-cost business consulting, training workshops, and print resources. Take advantage of your tax dollars at work!

Alan Weiss
summitconsulting.com

> Alan Weiss, author of *Million Dollar Consulting* among other titles, is the consultant's consultant. While he addresses much of his advice to speakers and consultants, it can be applied to any professional service. His web site includes a number of free resources, including business templates, articles, and newsletters.

Appendix B: Recommended Books for Reluctant Entrepreneurs

These are (mostly) books mentioned in *The Reluctant Entrepreneur* that I have found useful over the years of running my business. They have served to inspire me, guide me, give me tools, and make me laugh.

Allen, David. *Getting Things Done: The Art of Stress-Free Productivity*. New York: Viking, 2001. (Mentioned in Chapter 6 and Chapter 11.)

Ban Breathnach, Sarah. *Simple Abundance: A Daybook of Comfort and Joy*. New York: Grand Central Publishing, 1995. (Mentioned in Chapter 6.)

Cain, Susan. *Quiet: The Power of Introverts in a World That Can't Stop Talking*. New York: Crown Publishers, 2012. (Included here because many of us reluctant entrepreneurs are introverts.)

Fine, Debra. *The Fine Art of Small Talk: How To Start a Conversation, Keep It Going, Build Networking Skills, and Leave a Positive Impression.* New York: Hyperion, 2005. (Mentioned in Chapter 10.)

Fine, Debra. *The Fine Art of the Big Talk: How to Win Clients, Deliver Great Presentations, and Solve Conflicts at Work.* New York: Hyperion, 2008. (Mentioned in Chapter 10.)

Jantsch, John. *Duct Tape Marketing: The World's Most Practical Small Business Marketing Guide.* Nashville: Nelson Business, 2011. (Jantsch provides marketing consulting for small businesses and entrepreneurs, and offers useful, often contrarian, advice.)

Stein, Garth. *The Art of Racing in the Rain: A Novel.* New York: Harper, 2008. (Mentioned in Chapter 11.)

Tan, Chade-Meng. *Search Inside Yourself: The Unexpected Path to Achieving Success, Happiness (and World Peace)* New York: HarperOne, 2012. (A delightful book on cultivating emotional intelligence, written by an early Google engineer.)

Van Yoder, Stephen. *Get Slightly Famous: Become a Celebrity in Your Field and Attract More Business with Less Effort.* 2nd edition. Berkeley, CA: Bay Tree Publishing, 2007. (Mentioned in Chapter 9.)

Ware, Bronnie. *The Top Five Regrets of the Dying: A Life Transformed by the Dearly Departing.* Carlsbad, CA: Hay House, 2012. (Mentioned in Chapter 2.)

Writer's Market (annual). Cincinnati: Writer's Digest. (Mentioned in Chapter 10.)

Acknowledgements

> "But I don't want to go among mad people," Alice remarked.
> "Oh, you can't help that," said the Cat: "We're all mad here.
> I'm mad. You're mad."
>
> LEWIS CARROLL, FROM *ALICE'S ADVENTURES IN WONDERLAND*

First, many thanks to my coaching clients, who have shared their dreams, fears, and wonderings about their businesses with me. I have had the privilege of seeing the wide range of approaches to making a living, and I appreciate the opportunity to help my clients create businesses they love. Thank you for letting me share your perspective of what it means to be an entrepreneur—reluctant or not.

My editor and collaborator, Verna Wilder, is responsible for shepherding this book from thought to publication. Her kind, sharp, loving attention improved it immeasurably, and our face-to-face meetings kept me focused and energized. I am grateful beyond words for her presence in my life; who knew that a chance conversation would turn into such a fun project?

I am thankful for the wise counsel I get from my brain trust of Marcy Phelps and Kim Dority. We encourage each other to dream big dreams and then challenge each other to take the steps needed to bring those dreams to reality. I appreciate the insights and clarity that come from each of our meetings.

Many thanks to Marcy, Kim, Julie Colwell, and Bob Berkman, all of whom read a draft of this book and offered thoughtful insights and suggestions for improvement. The book is better because of their comments, and I am grateful that four such busy entrepreneurs were so generous with their time and attention.

And thanks beyond measure to Lin Harden, who has so enriched my life with her love, joy, and wisdom. Every day, I'm grateful that we finally found each other.

About the Author

> "She generally gave herself very good advice,
> (though she very seldom followed it)."
>
> LEWIS CARROLL, FROM *ALICE'S ADVENTURES IN WONDERLAND*

Mary Ellen Bates is a no-longer-reluctant entrepreneur who loves what she does. After working as a corporate librarian for a decade, she gave up the boredom of a steady paycheck in 1991 and launched Bates Information Services. Through much trial and error, she discovered that it is possible to run a business and have fun in the process.

Mary Ellen's secret is to constantly evolve to meet the current needs and concerns of her clients. Back in the dark days before the web, her main focus was using specialized online databases to conduct research for telecom companies. Now she provides business analysis for a wide range of corporate clients as well as consulting services for the information industry.

She was surprised to find that writing and public speaking—both of which were part of her initial marketing plan—have become a source of pleasure rather than anguish. She has been a keynote speaker at conferences around the world (in fifteen countries at last count) and has written seven books and hundreds of articles. One of Mary Ellen's passions is helping people explore ways to live life more fully, and the most rewarding aspect of her business is the coaching she offers to both new and long-time entrepreneurs.

Mary Ellen lives near Boulder, Colorado, with her wife and two dogs.

Made in the USA
San Bernardino, CA
20 February 2015